THE LIFE
OF
BUDDHA

THE LIFE
of
BUDDHA

*According to the Legends of
Ancient India*

By

A. FERDINAND HEROLD

Translated from the French by

PAUL C. BLUM

Decorations by Mac Harshberger

TOKYO

CHARLES E. TUTTLE COMPANY

1954

Representatives
Continental Europe: BOXERBOOKS, INC., *Zurich*
British Isles: PRENTICE-HALL INTERNATIONAL, INC., *London*
Australasia: PAUL FLESCH & CO., PTY. LTD., *Melbourne*
Canada: HURTIG PUBLISHERS, *Edmonton*

Published by the Charles E. Tuttle Company, Inc.
of Rutland, Vermont & Tokyo, Japan
with editorial offices at
Suido 1-chome, 2-6, Bunkyo-ku, Tokyo, Japan

© *1954 by Charles E. Tuttle Co., Inc.*

Library of Congress Catalog Card No. 55-12748

International Standard Book No. 0-8048-0382-X

First printing, 1955
Tenth printing, 1974

PRINTED IN JAPAN

FOREWORD

This Life of Buddha is not a work of fiction, and I think it would be well to mention the books, both ancient and modern, which I have most frequently consulted.

I have, for the most part, relied upon the LALITA-VISTARA. This book is a jumbled collection of legends and scholastic dissertations, and yet in these pages are preserved many precious traditions regarding the Buddha's origin, his childhood and his youth, and here, likewise, we are told of his early education and of his first deeds.

I have also made great use of an excellent poem, the BUDDHACARITA of Asvaghosa. In a few of the chapters I have repeated the lines almost word for word. The text of the BUDDHACARITA was edited by E. B. Cowell.

In the Life, I have interpolated several JATAKAS. These are stories in which the Buddha recalls his former lives. Some of them will be found in a vast collection, the AVADANASATAKA.

Two modern books: LE BOUDDHA, by H. Oldenberg, translated by A. Foucher, and the HISTOIRE DU BOUDDHISME DANS L'INDE, by

FOREWORD

H. Kern, translated by Gédéon Huet, have also been very useful to me; as well as other works that have appeared in scientific reviews. Thus, for the touching story of Visvantara, I am indebted to a sogdian version published by R. Gauthiot in the JOURNAL ASIATIQUE.

Finally, I would be guilty of the deepest ingratitude if I did not publicly thank my old friend Sylvain Lévi for his generous and kindly advice.

And may the reader find of interest this marvellous story of Prince Siddhartha who, through meditation, was able to attain supreme wisdom.

A. F. HEROLD

TABLE OF CONTENTS

PART ONE

TABLE OF CONTENTS
PART TWO

TABLE OF CONTENTS

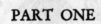

PART ONE

1

SERENE and magnificent was this city where once had dwelt the great hermit Kapila. It seemed to be built out of some fragment of the sky: the walls were like clouds of light, and the houses and gardens radiated a divine splendor. Precious stones glistened everywhere. Within its gates darkness was as little known as poverty. At night, when silver moonbeams fingered each turret, the city was like a pond of lilies; by day, when the terraces were bathed in golden sunshine, the city was like a river of lotuses.

King Suddhodana reigned in Kapilavastu; he was its brightest ornament. He was kindly and generous, modest and just. He pursued his bravest enemies, and they fell before him in battle like elephants struck down by Indra; and as darkness is dissipated by the sharp rays of the sun, even so were the wicked vanquished by his radiant glory. He brought light into the world, and he pointed out the true path to those who were close to him. His great wisdom gained for him many friends, many courageous, discerning friends, and as starlight in-

3

tensifies the brightness of the moon, so did their brilliance enhance his splendor.

Suddhodana, king of the Sakya race, had wed many queens. His favorite among these was Maya.

She was very beautiful. It was as if the Goddess Lakshmi herself had strayed into the world. When she spoke, it was like the song of birds in the spring, and her words were sweet and pleasant. Her hair was the color of the black bee; her forehead was as chaste as a diamond; her eyes as cool as a young blue-lotus leaf; and no frown ever marred the exquisite curve of her brows.

She was virtuous. She desired the happiness of her subjects; she was attentive to the pious precepts of her teachers. She was truthful, and her conduct was exemplary.

King Suddhodana and Queen Maya lived quietly and happily in Kapilavastu.

One day, the queen bathed and perfumed her body, then attired herself in a delicate, colorful robe and covered her arms with jewels. Golden bangles tinkled about her ankles, and her face was radiant with happiness as she sought the king's presence.

Suddhodana was seated in a great hall. Sweet music was lulling his tranquil reverie. Maya took the seat on his right, and she said to him:

"Deign to listen, my lord. Deign to grant the

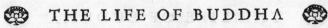

favor I have to ask of you, O protector of the earth."

"Speak, my queen," replied Suddhodana. "What is this favor?"

"My lord, there is great suffering in the world, and I look with compassion on all who suffer. I would be helpful to my fellow-creatures; I would close my mind to evil thoughts. And since I shall forbear doing and thinking evil, since I am thus kind to myself, I would be helpful, I would be kind to others, too. I will put aside pride, O king, and I will not listen to the voice of evil desire. I will never utter a vain or dishonorable word. My lord, henceforth I will lead a life of austerity; I will fast; and I will never bear ill will or commit wickedness, suffer anxiety or hatred, know anger or covetousness. I will be satisfied with my lot; I will forswear deceit and envy; I will be pure; I will walk in the straight path; and I will practise virtue. And because of these things my eyes are now smiling, because of these things my lips are now joyous."

She paused a moment. The king gazed at her in tender admiration. She continued:

"My lord, I ask you to respect my austere life. Do not enter the dim forest of desire; allow me to observe the holy law of abstinence. I shall repair to those apartments that are in the lofty reaches of the

5

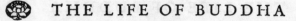

palace, and there, where the swans build their nests, have prepared for me a couch strewn with flowers, a soft, perfumed couch. My maidens shall attend to my wants, and you may dismiss the eunuchs, the guards and all vulgar servants. I would be spared the sight of ugliness, the sound of revelry and the odor of things unpleasant."

She said no more. The king replied:

"So let it be! The favor you ask, I grant."

And he commanded:

"Up there, in the lofty reaches of the palace, where the air throbs with the song of the swans, let the queen, resplendent in gold and precious stones, rest on a couch of rare flowers; and let there be music. And to her maidens, gathered about her, she will be like a daughter of the Gods in some celestial garden!"

The queen rose.

"It is well, my lord," said she. "But hear me further. Free your prisoners. Give generously to the poor. Let men and women and children be happy! Be merciful, O king, and, that the world may be joyous, be a father to all living creatures!"

She then left the hall and went to the top of the royal palace.

It was the advent of spring. Birds darted and wheeled above the terraces; birds sang in the trees. The gardens were in flower; on the surface of the

6

ponds, the lotus buds were unfolding. And, as the queen sought her bower, the piping note of flutes and the deeper harmony of strings resounded of their own accord, and a refulgent glory appeared over the palace, a glory so perfect that the sunlight turned to shadow.

THE same hour that spring was born, a dream came to Maya as she slept.

She saw a young elephant descending from the sky. It had six great tusks; it was as white as the snow on mountain-tops. Maya saw it enter her womb, and thousands of Gods suddenly appeared before her. They praised her with immortal songs, and Maya understood that nevermore would she know disquietude or hatred or anger.

Then she awoke. She was happy; it was a happiness she had never felt before. Arising, she arrayed herself in bright colors, and, followed by her most beautiful maidens, she passed through the palace-gates. She walked in the gardens until she came to a little wood, where she found a shaded seat. Then she sent two of her maidens to King Suddhodana with this message: "That the king should come to the wood; Queen Maya wishes to see him and will await him there."

The king promptly complied. He left the hall where, with the help of his counsellors, he had been administering justice to the inhabitants of the city.

He walked toward the wood, but, as he was about to enter, a strange feeling came over him. His limbs faltered, his hands trembled and tears welled from his eyes. And he thought:

"Never, not even in the heat of battle when fighting my bravest enemies, have I felt as profoundly disturbed as at this moment. Why is it I can not enter the wood where the queen awaits me? Can anyone explain my agitation?"

Whereupon a great voice thundered in the sky:

"Be happy, King Suddhodana, worthiest of the Sakyas! He who seeks supreme knowledge is about to come into the world. He has chosen your family to be his family because of its fame, good fortune and virtue, and for mother he has chosen the noblest of all women, your wife, Queen Maya. Be happy, King Suddhodana! He who seeks supreme knowledge would fain be your son!"

The king knew that the Gods were speaking, and he rejoiced. Regaining his serenity, he entered the wood where Maya awaited him.

He saw her; quietly, without arrogance, he asked:

"Why did you send for me? What do you wish?"

The queen told him of the dream she had had; then added:

"My lord, there are brahmans who are clever at interpreting dreams. Send for them. They will

9

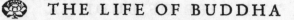

know if the palace has been visited by good or evil, and if we should rejoice or mourn."

The king agreed, and brahmans familiar with the mystery of dreams were summoned to the palace. When they had heard Maya's story they spoke in this manner:

"A great joy is to be yours, O king, O queen. A son will be born to you, distinguished by the favor of the Gods. If, one day, he should renounce royalty, leave the palace, cast love aside; if, seized with compassion for the worlds, he should live the wandering life of a monk, he will deserve marvellous praise, he will richly deserve magnificent gifts. He will be adored by the worlds, for he will give them that which they hunger after. O master, O mistress, your son will be a Buddha!"

The brahmans withdrew. The king and queen looked at each other, and their faces were radiant with happiness and peace. Suddhodana then ordered that alms be distributed to the poor in Kapilavastu; and food was given to the hungry, drink to the thirsty, and the women received flowers and perfume. Maya became the object of their veneration; the sick crowded her path, and when she extended her right hand they were cured. The blind saw, the deaf heard, the dumb spoke, and when the dying touched a blade of grass she had gathered they recovered at once their health and their

10

strength. And above the city a ceaseless melody was borne on the wind, exquisite flowers rained from the sky, and songs of gratitude rose on the air around the palace walls.

$\gtrless$

MONTHS passed. Then, one day, the queen knew that the time was approaching for her son to be born. She went to King Suddhodana, and she said to him:

"My lord, I would wander through the happy gardens. Birds are singing in the trees, and the air is bright with flower-dust. I would wander through the happy gardens."

"But it will weary you, O queen," replied Suddhodana. "Are you not afraid?"

"The innocent being that I carry in my womb must be born amid the innocence of budding flowers. No, I will go, O master, I will go into the flower-gardens."

The king yielded to Maya's wish. He said to his servants:

"Go into the gardens and deck them out in silver and in gold. Drape the trees with precious hangings. Let everything be magnificent, for the queen will pass."

Then he addressed Maya:

"Array yourself. to-day, in great splendor, O

12

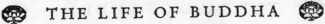

Maya. Ride in a gorgeous palanquin; let your most beautiful maidens carry you. Order your servants to use rare perfumes; have them wear ropes of pearls and bracelets of precious stones; have them carry lutes and drums and flutes, and sing sweet songs that would delight the Gods themselves."

Suddhodana was obeyed, and when the queen reached the palace-gates the guards greeted her with joyous cries. Bells peeled gaily, peacocks spread their gorgeous tail-feathers, and the song of swans throbbed in the air.

They came to a wood where the trees were in bloom, and Maya ordered them to set down the palanquin. She stepped out and began wandering about, aimlessly. She was happy. And behold! she found a rare tree, the branches drooping under their burden of blossoms. She went up to it; gracefully extending her hand, she drew down a branch. Suddenly, she stood very still. She smiled, and the maidens who were near her received a lovely child into their arms.

At that same moment all that was alive in the world trembled with joy. The earth quivered. Songs and the patter of dancing feet echoed in the sky. Trees of all seasons burst into flower, and ripe fruit hung from the branches. A pure, serene light appeared in the sky. The sick were rid of their suffering. The hungry were satisfied. Those to

13

whom wine had played false became sober. Madmen recovered their reason, the weak their strength,
the poor their wealth. Prisons opened their gates.
The wicked were cleansed of all evil.

One of Maya's maidens hastened to King
Suddhodana and joyously exclaimed:

"My lord, my lord, a son is born to you, a son
who will bring great glory to your house!"

He was speechless. But his face was radiant with
joy, and he knew great happiness.

Presently he summoned all the Sakyas, and he
commanded them to accompany him into the
garden where the child had been born. They
obeyed, and, with a host of brahmans in attend-
ance, they formed a noble retinue as they gravely
followed the king.

When he came near the child, the king made a
deep obeisance, and he said:

"Do you bow as I bow before the prince, to
whom I give the name Siddhartha."

They all bowed, and the brahmans, inspired by
the Gods, then sang:

"All creatures are happy, and they are no longer
rough, those roads travelled by men, for he is born,
he who gives happiness: he will bring happiness
into the world. In the darkness a great light has
dawned, the sun and the moon are like dying em-
bers, for he is born, he who gives light: he will

bring light into the world. The blind see, the deaf hear, the foolish have recovered their reason, for he is born, he who restores sight, and restores hearing, and restores the mind: he will bring sight, he will bring hearing, he will bring reason into the world. Perfumed zephyrs ease the suffering of mankind, for he is born, he who heals: he will bring health into the world. Flames are no longer pitiless, the flow of rivers has been stayed, the earth has trembled gently: he will be the one to see the truth."

bring light into the world. The blind, Asita added, shall recover their sight, for he is come; he who tears asunder and casts off...

卐

THE great hermit Asita, whose austerities were pleasing to the Gods, heard of the birth of him who was to save mankind from the torment of rebirth. In his thirst for the true law, he came ·to the palace of King Suddhodana and gravely approached the women's quarters. His years and his learning lent him great dignity.

The king showed him the courtesies that custom prescribed and addressed him in a seemly manner:

"Happy, indeed, am I! Truly, this child of mine will enjoy distinguished favor, for the venerable Asita has come purposely to see me. Command me. What must I do? I am your disciple, your servant."

The hermit, his eyes shining with the light of joy, gravely spoke these words:

"This has happened to you, O noble, generous and hospitable king, because you love duty and because you are ever kind to those who are wise and to those who are full of years. This has happened to you because your ancestors, though rich in land

16

and rich in gold, were above all rich in virtue.
Know the reason for my coming, O king, and rejoice. In the air I heard a divine voice speaking
and it said: 'A son has been born to the king of the
Sakyas, a son who will have the true knowledge.'
I heard these words, and I came, and my eyes shall
now behold the glory of the Sakyas."

Overwhelmed with joy, the king went to fetch
the child. Taking him from his nurse's breast, he
showed him to the aged Asita.

The hermit noticed that the king's son bore the
marks of omnipotence. His gaze hovered over the
child, and presently his lashes were wet with tears.
Then he sighed and turned his eyes to the sky.

The king saw that Asita was weeping, and he
began to fear for his son. He questioned the old
man:

"You say, O venerable man, that my son's body
differs little from that of a God. You say that his
birth was a wondrous thing, that in the future
his glory will be supreme, yet you look at him
with eyes that are filled with tears. Is his life, then,
to be a fragile thing? Was he born only to bring
me sorrow? Must this new branch wither before it has burst into flower? Speak, O saintly man,
speak quickly; you know the great love a father
bears his son."

"Be not distressed, O king," replied the hermit.

17

"What I have told you is true: this child will know great glory. If I weep, it is for myself. My life draws to a close and he is born, he who will destroy the evil of rebirth. He will surrender sovereign power, he will master his passions, he will understand truth, and error will disappear in the world before the light of his knowledge, even as night flees before the spears of the sun. From the sea of evil, from the stinging spray of sickness, from the surge and swell of old age, from the angry waves of death, from these will he rescue the suffering world, and together they will sail away in the great ship of knowledge. He will know where it takes its rise, that swift, wonderful, beneficent river, the river of duty; he will reveal its course, and those who are tortured by thirst will come and drink of its waters. To those tormented by sorrow, to those enslaved by the senses, to those wandering in the forest of existences like travellers who have lost their way, he will point out the road to salvation. To those burning with the fire of passion, he will be the cloud that brings refreshing rain; armed with the true law, he will go to the prison of desires where all creatures languish, and he will break down the evil gates. For he who will have perfect understanding will set the world free. Therefore do not grieve, O king. He alone is to be pitied who will not hear the voice of your son, and that is why

18

THE LIFE OF BUDDHA

I weep, I who, in spite of my austerities, in spite of my meditations, will never know his message and his law. Yes, even he is to be pitied who ascends to the loftiest gardens of the sky."

19

§

THEY pleased Suddhodana at first, these words of Asita's, and he pondered them. "So my son will live, and live gloriously," he thought, but then he became anxious. For it had been said that the prince would renounce royalty, that he would lead the life of a hermit, and did that not mean that at his death Suddhodana's family would cease?

But his anxiety was short-lived, for since the birth of Siddhartha the king could undertake nothing that did not prosper. Like a great river whose waters are swollen by many tributaries, each day new riches poured into his treasury; the stables were too small to hold the horses and elephants that were presented to him, and he was constantly surrounded by a host of loyal friends. The kingdom was rich in fertile lands, and sleek, fatted cattle grazed in the meadows. Women bore their children without suffering; men lived at peace with their neighbors, and happiness and tranquillity reigned in the land of Kapilavastu.

But the joy that had come to Maya proved

too sweet. It soon became unbearable. The earth knew her as a mother but seven days; then she died and ascended to the sky, to be received among the Gods.

Maya had a sister, Mahaprajapati, who in beauty and virtue was almost her equal. The prince was given into Mahaprajapati's care, and she looked after his wants as tenderly as if he were her own child. And like fire fanned by an auspicious wind, like the moon, queen of the stars in the luminous skies, like the morning sun rising over the mountains in the East, Siddhartha grew in strength and stature.

Everyone now delighted in bringing him precious gifts. They gave him toys that would amuse a child of his age: tiny animals, deer and elephants, horses, cows, birds and fish, and little chariots; and they were toys made not of wood or of clay but of gold and of precious stones. And they brought him costly materials and rare gems, pearl necklaces and jewelled bracelets.

One day, while he was playing in a garden not far from the city, Mahaprajapati thought, "It is time I taught him to wear necklaces and bracelets," and she ordered the servants to bring the jewels that had been given to him. She clasped them around his arms and his neck, but it was as if he wore none at all. The gold and the precious stones

21

seemed dull and lifeless, so brilliant was the light he diffused. And the Goddess who lived among the flowers of that garden came to Mahaprajapati and said:

"If the earth were made of gold, a single ray of light emanating from this child, the world's future guide, would be enough to dull its splendor. The light of the stars and the light of the moon, yes, even the light of the sun, are dimmed by his refulgence. And would you have him wear jewels, baubles crudely fashioned by jewellers and goldsmiths? Woman, remove those necklaces, take off those bracelets. They are only fit to be worn by slaves; give them to the slaves. This child will have his thoughts; they are gems of a purer water."

Mahaprajapati gave heed to the words of the Goddess. She unclasped the bracelets and the necklaces, and she never wearied of admiring the prince.

The time came to take Siddhartha to the temple of the Gods. By the king's command, the streets of the city and the public squares were superbly decorated; drums were sounded and bells joyously rung. While Mahaprajapati was dressing him in his richest apparel, the child asked:

"Mother, where are you taking me?"

"To the temple of the Gods, my son," she replied.

The child smiled and quietly went with her to meet his father.

It was a magnificent sight. In the procession were brahmans from the city, warriors and all the chief merchants. A host of guards followed, and the Sakyas surrounded the chariot that bore the prince and the king. In the streets the air was heavy with incense, flowers were strewn in their path, and the people waved flags and streamers as they passed.

They arrived at the temple. The king took Siddhartha by the hand and led him to the hall where stood the statues of the Gods. As the child stepped across the threshold the statues came to life, and all the Gods, Siva, Skanda, Vishnu, Kuvera, Indra, Brahma, descended from their pedestals and fell at his feet. And they sang:

"Meru, king of the mountains, does not bow before a grain of wheat; the Ocean does not bow before a pool of rainwater; the Sun does not bow before a glowworm; he who will have the true knowledge does not bow before the Gods. Like the grain of wheat, like the pool of rainwater, like the glowworm is the man or the God with stubborn pride; like Meru mountain, like the Ocean, like the Sun is he who will have supreme knowledge. Let the world pay him homage, and the world will be set free!"

6

THE prince grew older, and the time came for him to study with the teacher who instructed the young Sakyas in the art of writing. This teacher was called Visvamitra.

Siddhartha was entrusted to his care. He was given, to write on, a tablet of gilded sandal-wood, set round with precious stones. When he had it in his hands, he asked:

"Which script, master, would you have me learn?"

And he enumerated the sixty-four varieties of script. Then again he asked:

"Master, which of the sixty-four would you have me learn?"

Visvamitra made no answer: he was struck dumb with astonishment. Finally, he replied:

"I see, my lord, that there is nothing I can teach you. Of the scripts you mentioned, some are known to me only by name, and others are unknown to me even by name. It is I who should sit at your feet and learn. No, my lord, there is nothing I can teach you."

24

He was smiling, and the prince returned his affectionate glance.

Upon leaving Visvamitra, the prince went into the country and started walking toward a village. On the way, he stopped to watch some peasants working in the fields, then he entered a meadow where stood a clump of trees. They attracted him, for it was noon and very hot. The prince went and sat down in the shade of a tree; there, he began to ponder, and he was soon lost in meditation.

Five itinerant hermits passed near the meadow. They saw the prince meditating, and they wondered:

"Is he a God, he who is seated there, resting? Could he be the God of riches, or the God of love? Could he be Indra, bearer of thunder, or the shepherd Krishna?"

But they heard a voice saying to them:

"The splendor of the Gods would pale before the splendor of this Sakya who sits under the tree and ponders majestic truths!"

Whereupon they all exclaimed:

"Verily, he who sits and meditates under the tree bears the marks of omnipotence; he will doubtless become the Buddha!"

Then they sang his praises, and the first one said: "To a world consumed by an evil fire, he has come like a lake. His law will refresh the world."

25

The second one said: "To a world darkened by ignorance, he has come like a torch. His law will bring light into the world."

The third one said: "Over the sea of suffering, that sea so difficult to sail, he has come like a ship. His law will bring the world safely into harbor."

The fourth one said: "To those bound in chains of evil, he has come like a redeemer. His law will set the world free."

The fifth one said: "To those tormented by old age and sickness, he has come like a savior. His law will bring deliverance from birth and death."

Three times they bowed, then continued on their way.

In the meanwhile, King Suddhodana wondered what had become of the prince, and he sent many servants out to search for him. One of them found him absorbed in meditation. The servant drew near, then suddenly stopped, overcome with admiration. For the shadows of all the trees had lengthened, except of that tree under which the prince was seated. Its shadow had not moved; it still sheltered him.

The servant ran back to the palace of the king.

"My lord," he cried, "I have seen your son; he is meditating under a tree whose shadow has not moved, whereas the shadows of all the other trees have moved and lengthened."

26

Suddhodana left the palace and followed the servant to where his son was seated. Weeping for joy, he said to himself:

"He is as beautiful as fire on a mountain-top. He dazzles me. He will be the light of the world, and my limbs tremble when I see him thus in meditation."

The king and his servant dared neither move nor speak. But some children passed by, drawing a little chariot after them. They were making a noise. The servant said to them, in a whisper:

"You must not make a noise."

"Why?" asked the children.

"See him who meditates under the tree? That is Prince Siddhartha. The shadow of the tree has not left him. Do not disturb him, children; do you not see that he has the brilliance of the sun?"

But the prince awoke from his meditations. He rose and approaching his father, he said to him:

"We must stop working in the fields, father; we must seek the great truths."

And he returned to Kapilavastu.

7

SUDDHODANA kept thinking of what Asita had told him. He did not want his family to die out, and he said to himself:

"I will arouse in my son a desire for pleasure; then, perhaps, I shall have grandchildren, and they shall prosper."

So he sent for the prince, and he spoke to him in these words:

"My child, you are at an age when it would be well to think of marriage. If there is some maid that pleases you, tell me."

Siddhartha replied:

"Give me seven days to consider, father. In seven days you shall have my answer."

And he mused:

"Endless evil, I know, comes of desire. The trees that grow in the forest of desire have their roots in suffering and strife, and their leaves are poisonous. Desire burns like fire and wounds like a sword. I am not one of those who seek the company of women; it is my lot to live in the silence of the woods. There, through meditation, my mind will

find peace, and I shall know happiness. But does not the lotus grow and flourish even amid the tangle of swamp-flowers? Have there not been men with wives and sons who found wisdom? Those who, before me, have sought supreme knowledge spent many years in the company of women. And when the time came to leave them for the delights of meditation, theirs was but a greater joy. I shall follow their example."

He thought of the qualities he would value most highly in a woman. Then, on the seventh day, he returned to his father.

"Father," said he, "she whom I shall marry must be a woman of rare merit. If you find one endowed with the natural gifts I shall enumerate, you may give her to me in marriage."

And he said:

"She whom I shall marry will be in the bloom of youth; she whom I shall marry will have the flower of beauty; yet her youth will not make her vain, nor will her beauty make her proud. She whom I shall marry will have a sister's affection, a mother's tenderness, for all living creatures. She will be sweet and truthful, and she will not know envy. Never, not even in her dreams, will she think of any other man but her husband. She will never use haughty language; her manner will be unassuming; she will be as meek as a slave. She will not covet that which

29

belongs to others; she will make no inconsiderate demands, and she will be satisfied with her lot. She will care nothing for wines, and sweets will not tempt her. She will be insensible to music and perfume; she will be indifferent to plays and festivals. She will be kind to my attendants and to her maidens. She will be the first to awaken and the last to fall asleep. She whom I shall marry will be pure in body, in speech and in thought."

And he added:

"Father, if you know a maid who possesses these qualities, you may give her to me in marriage."

The king summoned the household priest. He enumerated the qualities the prince sought in the woman he would marry, then:

"Go," said he, "go, brahman. Visit all the homes of Kapilavastu; observe the young girls and question them. And if you find one to possess the necessary qualities, bring her to the prince, even though she be of the lowest caste. For it is not rank nor riches my son seeks, but virtue."

The priest scoured the city of Kapilavastu. He entered the houses, he saw the young girls, he cleverly questioned them; but not one could he find worthy of Prince Siddhartha. Finally, he came to the home of Dandapani who was of the Sakya family. Dandapani had a daughter named Gopa. At the very sight of her, the priest's heart rejoiced, for she was beautiful and full of grace. He spoke a few words to her, and he doubted no longer.

The priest returned to King Suddhodana. "My lord," he exclaimed, "I have found a maid worthy of your son."

"Where did you find her?" asked the king.

"She is the daughter of the Sakya, Dandapani," the brahman replied.

Though he had great confidence in his household priest, Suddhodana hesitated to summon Gopa and Dandapani. "Even the wisest men can make mistakes," he thought. "The brahman may be exaggerating her perfections. I must put the daughter of Dandapani to a further test, and my son himself shall judge her."

He had many jewels made out of gold and silver, and by royal command a herald was sent through the streets of Kapilavastu, crying:

"On the seventh day from this day, Prince Siddhartha, son of King Suddhodana, will present gifts to the young girls of the city. So may all the young girls appear at the palace on the seventh day!"

On the day announced, the prince sat on a throne in the great hall of the palace. All the young girls of the city were present, and they filed before him. To each one he presented a jewel, but, as they approached the throne, his striking beauty so intimidated them that they lowered their gaze or turned their heads away. They hardly took the time to receive their presents; some were even in such haste to leave that they merely touched the gift with the tips of their fingers, and it fell to the floor.

Gopa was the last one to appear. She advanced fearlessly, without even blinking her eyes. But the prince had not a single jewel left. Gopa smiled and said to him:

"Prince, in what way have I offended you?"

"You have not offended me," replied Siddhartha.

"Then why do you treat me with disdain?"

"I do not treat you with disdain," he replied. "You are the last one, and I have no jewel to give you."

But suddenly he remembered that on his finger he was wearing a ring of great value. He took it off and handed it to the young girl.

She would not take the ring.

She said, "Prince, must I accept this ring from you?"

"It was mine," replied the prince, "and you must accept it."

"No," said she, "I would not deprive you of your jewels. It is for me, rather, to give you a jewel."

And she left.

When the king heard of this incident he was elated.

"Gopa, alone, could face my son," he thought;

"she alone is worthy of him. Gopa, who would not accept the ring that you took from your finger, Gopa, O my son, will be your fairest jewel."

And he summoned Gopa's father to the palace.

"Friend," said he, "the time has come for my son Siddhartha to marry. I believe your daughter Gopa has found favor in his eyes. Will you marry her to my son?"

Dandapani did not answer at once. He hesitated, and again the king asked him:

"Will you marry your daughter to my son?"

Then Dandapani said:

"My lord, your son has been brought up in luxury; he has never been outside the palace-gates; his physical and intellectual abilities have never been proven. You know that the Sakyas only marry their daughters to men who are skillful and strong, brave and wise. How can I give my daughter to your son who, so far, has shown a taste only for indolence?"

These words disturbed King Suddhodana. He asked to see the prince. Siddhartha came immediately.

"Father," said he, "you look very sad. What has happened?"

The king did not know how to tell him what Dandapani had so bluntly expressed. He remained silent.

The prince repeated:

"Father, you look very sad. What has happened?"

"Do not ask me," replied Suddhodana.

"Father, you are sad, what has happened?"

"It is a painful subject; I would rather not speak of it."

"Explain yourself, father. It is always well to be explicit."

The king finally decided to relate the interview he had had with Dandapani. When he had finished, the prince began to laugh.

"My lord," said he, "you are needlessly disturbed. Do you believe there is anyone in Kapilavastu who is my superior in strength or in intellect? Summon all who are famous for their attainments in any field whatsoever; command them to measure their skill with mine, and I shall show you what I can do."

The king recovered his serenity. He had it proclaimed throughout the city:

"That on the seventh day from this day, Prince Siddhartha will compete with all who excel in any field whatsoever."

On the day designated, all those who claimed to be skillful in the arts or in the sciences appeared at the palace. Dandapani was present, and he promised his daughter to the one, whether of noble or of humble birth, who would be victorious in the contests which were to take place.

First, a young man, who knew the rules of writing, sought to challenge the prince, but the learned Visvamitra stepped before the assembly and said: "Young man, such a contest would be futile. You are already defeated. The prince was still a child when he was placed in my care; I was to teach him the art of writing. But he already knew sixty-four varieties of script! He knew certain varieties that were unknown to me even by name!"

Visvamitra's testimony was enough to give the prince a victory in the art of writing.

Then they sought to test his knowledge of numbers. It was decided that a certain Sakya named Arjuna, who had time and again solved intricate problems, would act as judge in the contest.

One young man claimed to be an excellent mathematician, and to him Siddhartha addressed a question, but the young man was unable to reply.

"And yet it was an easy question," said the prince. "But here is one that is still easier; who will answer it?"

No one answered this second question.

"It is now your turn to examine me," said the prince.

They asked him questions that were considered

difficult, but he gave the answers even before they had finished stating the problem.

"Let Arjuna himself examine the prince!" came the cry from all sides.

Arjuna gave him the most intricate problems, and never once was Siddhartha at a loss for the correct solution.

They all marvelled at his knowledge of mathematics and were convinced that his intelligence had probed to the bottom of all the sciences. They then decided to challenge his athletic skill, but at jumping and at running he won with little effort, and at wrestling he had only to lay a finger upon his adversary, and he would fall to the ground.

Then they brought out the bows, and skillful archers placed their arrows in targets that were barely visible. But when it came the prince's turn to shoot, so great was his natural strength that he broke each bow as he drew it. Finally, the king sent guards to fetch a very ancient, very precious bow that was kept in the temple. No one within the memory of man had ever been able to draw or lift it. Siddhartha took the bow in his left hand, and with one finger of his right hand he drew it to him. Then he took as target a tree so distant that he alone could see it. The arrow pierced the tree, and, burying itself in the ground, disappeared. And there, where the arrow had entered the ground, a well formed, which was called the Well of the Arrow.

Everything seemed to be over, and they led toward the victor a huge white elephant on which, in triumph, he was to ride through Kapilavastu. But a young Sakya, Devadatta, who was very proud of his strength, seized the animal by the trunk and, in fun, struck it with his fist. The elephant fell to the ground.

The prince looked reprovingly at the young man and said:

"You have done an evil thing, Devadatta."

He touched the elephant with his foot, and it stood up and paid him homage.

Then they all acclaimed his glory, and the air rang with their cheers. Suddhodana was happy, and Dandapani, weeping with joy, exclaimed:

"Gopa, my daughter Gopa, be proud to be the wife of such a man."

8

PRINCE Siddhartha lived happily with his wife, the princess. And the king, whose love for his son now verged on adoration, took infinite care to spare him the sight of anything that might distress him. He built three magnificent palaces for him: one for the winter, one for the summer, and the third for the rainy season; and these he was forbidden ever to leave, to wander over the broad face of the earth.

In his palaces, white as autumn clouds and bright as the celestial chariots of the Gods and Goddesses, the prince drained the cup of pleasure. He led a life of voluptuous ease; he spent languid hours listening to music played by the princess and her maidens, and when beautiful, smiling dancers appeared before him and performed to the sound of golden kettle-drums, with delight he watched them as they swayed with a grace and loveliness rare even among the happy Apsarases.

Women cast furtive glances at him: their eyes boldly offered or archly pleaded, and their drooping lashes were a promise of ineffable delight. Their games amused him, their charms held him in thrall, and he was content to remain in these palaces so full of their laughter and song. For he knew nothing of old age and sickness; he knew nothing of death.

Suddhodana rejoiced at the life his son was leading, though his own conduct he judged with the utmost severity. He strove to keep his soul serene and pure; he refrained from doing evil, and he lavished gifts on those who were virtuous. He never yielded to indolence or pleasure; he was never burned by the poison of avarice. As wild horses are made to bear the yoke, even so did he subdue his passions, and in virtue he surpassed his kinsmen and his friends. The knowledge he acquired he placed at the service of his fellow-men, and he only studied those subjects that were useful to all. He not only sought the welfare of his own people but he also wanted the whole world to be happy. He purified his body with the water from the sacred ponds, and he purified his soul with the holy water of virtue. He never uttered a word that was pleasant and yet a lie; the truths he spoke never gave offense or pain. He tried to be just, and it was by honesty, not by force, that he defeated the pride of his enemies. He did not strike, he did not even look with anger upon those who deserved the penalty of death; instead, he gave them useful advice, and then their freedom.

The king was an example to all his subjects, and

Kapilavastu was the happiest and most virtuous of kingdoms.

Then beautiful Gopa bore the prince a son, and he was given the name of Rahula. King Suddhodana was happy to see his family prosper, and he was as proud of the birth of his grandson as he had been of the birth of his son.

He continued in the path of virtue, he lived almost like a hermit, and his actions were saintly; yet he kept urging on his beloved son to new pleasures, so great was his fear to see him leave the palace and the city and seek the austere refuge of the holy forests.

9

ONE day, some one spoke in the presence of the prince and told how the grass in the woods had become a tender green and the birds in the trees were singing of the spring, and how, in the ponds, the great lotuses were unfolding. Nature had broken the chains that winter had forged, and, around the city, those gardens so dear to young maidens were now gaily carpeted with flowers. Then, like an elephant too long confined in his stable, the prince had an irresistible desire to leave the palace.

The king learned of his son's desire, and he knew no way to oppose it.

"But," he thought, "Siddhartha must see nothing that will trouble the serenity of his soul; he must never suspect the evil there is in the world. I shall order the road cleared of beggars, of those who are sick and infirm and of all who suffer."

The city was decorated with garlands and streamers; a magnificent chariot was prepared, and the cripples, the aged and the beggars were ordered off the streets where the prince would pass.

When the time came, the king sent for his son, and there were tears in his eyes as he kissed him on the brow. His gaze lingered over him, then he said to him, "Go!" And with that word he gave him permission to leave the palace, though his heart spoke differently.

The prince's chariot was made of gold. It was drawn by four horses caparisoned in gold, and the charioteer held gold reins in his hands. Only the rich, the young and the beautiful were allowed on the streets he drove through, and they stopped to watch him as he went by. Some praised him for the kindness of his glance; others extolled his dignified bearing; still others exalted the beauty of his features; while many glorified his exuberant strength. And they all bowed before him, like banners dipped before the statue of some God.

The women in the houses heard the cries in the street. They awoke or left their household tasks and ran to the windows or quickly ascended to the terraces. And gazing at him in admiration, they murmured, "Happy the wife of such a man!"

And he, at the sight of the city's splendor, at the sight of the wealth of the men and the beauty of the women, felt a new joy pour into his soul.

But the Gods were jealous of the celestial felicity enjoyed by this city of the earth. They made an old man, and, in order to trouble Siddhartha's mind, they set him down on the road the prince was travelling.

The man was leaning on a staff; he was worn out and decrepit. His veins stood out on his body, his teeth chattered, and his skin was a maze of black wrinkles. A few dirty grey hairs hung from his scalp; his eyelids had no lashes and were red-rimmed; his head and limbs were palsied.

The prince saw this being, so different from the men around him. He gazed at him with sorrowful eyes, and he asked the charioteer:

"What is this man with grey hair and body so bent? He clings to his staff with scrawny hands, his eyes are dull and his limbs falter. Is he a monster? Has nature made him thus, or is it chance?"

The charioteer should not have answered, but the Gods confused his mind, and without understanding his mistake he said:

"That which mars beauty, which ruins vigor, which causes sorrow and kills pleasure, that which weakens the memory and destroys the senses is old age. It has seized this man and broken him. He, too, was once a child, nursing at his mother's breast; he, too, once crawled upon the floor; he grew, he was young, he had strength and beauty; then he reached the twilight of his years, and now you see him, the ruin that is old age."

The prince was deeply moved. He asked:

"Will that be my fate, also?"

The charioteer replied:

"My lord, youth will also leave you some day; to you, too, will come troublesome old age. Time saps our strength and steals our beauty."

The prince shuddered like a bull at the sound of thunder. He uttered a deep sigh and shook his head. His eyes wandered from the wretched man to the happy crowds, and he spoke these solemn words:

"So old age destroys memory and beauty and strength in man, and yet the world is not frantic with terror! Turn your horses around, O charioteer; let us return to our homes. How can I delight in gardens and flowers when my eyes can only see old age, when my mind can only think of old age?"

The prince returned to his palace, but nowhere could he find peace. He wandered through the halls, murmuring, "Old age, oh, old age!" and in his heart there was no longer any joy.

He decided, nevertheless, to ride once more through the city.

But the Gods made a man afflicted with a loathsome disease, and they set him down on the road Siddhartha had taken.

Siddhartha saw the sick man; he stared at him, and he asked the charioteer:

"What is this man with a swollen paunch? His emaciated arms hang limp, he is deathly pale and pitiful cries escape from his lips. He gasps for breath; see, he staggers and jostles the bystanders; he is falling. . . . Charioteer, charioteer, what is this man?"

The charioteer answered:

"My lord, this man knows the torment of sickness, for he has the king's evil. He is weakness itself; yet he, too, was once healthy and strong!"

The prince looked at the man with pity, and he asked again:

"Is this affliction peculiar to this man, or are all creatures threatened with sickness?"

The charioteer answered:

"We, too, may be visited with a similar affliction, O prince. Sickness weighs heavily upon the world."

When he heard this painful truth, the prince began to tremble like a moonbeam reflected in the waves of the sea, and he uttered these words of bitterness and pity:

"Men see suffering and sickness, yet they never lose their self-confidence! Oh, how great must be their knowledge! They are constantly threatened with sickness, and they can still laugh and be merry! Turn your horses around, charioteer; our pleasure trip is ended; let us return to the palace. I have learned to fear sickness. My soul shuns pleasure and seems to close up like a flower deprived of light."

Wrapped in his painful thoughts, he returned to the palace.

King Suddhodana noticed his son's sombre mood. He asked why the prince no longer went out driving, and the charioteer told him what had happened. The king grieved; he already saw himself forsaken by the child he adored. He lost his usual composure and flew into a rage at the man whose duty it was to see that the streets were clear; he punished him, but so strong was his habit of being indulgent that the punishment was light. And the man was astonished at being thus upbraided, for he had seen neither the old man nor the sick man.

The king was more anxious now than ever before to keep his son from leaving the palace. He provided him with rare pleasures, but nothing, it seemed, could arouse Siddhartha. And the king thought, "I shall let him go out once more! Perhaps he will recover the joy he has lost."

He gave strict orders to have all cripples and all who were ill or aged driven out of the city. He even changed the prince's charioteer, and he felt certain that this time there would be nothing to trouble Siddhartha's soul.

But the jealous Gods made a corpse. Four men carried it, and others followed behind, weeping.

And the corpse, as well as the men who carried it and the men who were weeping, was visible only to the prince and to the charioteer.

And the king's son asked:

"What is he that is being carried by four men, followed by those others, wearing dark clothes and weeping?"

The charioteer should have held his peace, but it was the will of the Gods that he reply:

"My lord, he has neither intelligence nor feeling nor breath; he sleeps, without consciousness, like grass or a piece of wood; pleasure and suffering are meaningless to him now, and friend and enemy alike have deserted him."

The prince was troubled. He said, "Is this a condition peculiar to this man, or does this same end await all creatures?"

And the charioteer answered: "This same end awaits all creatures. Whether of humble or of noble birth, to every being who lives in this world, death comes inevitably."

Then Prince Siddhartha knew what death was. In spite of his fortitude, he shuddered. He had to lean against the chariot, and his words were full of distress:

"So to this does destiny lead all creatures! And yet, without fear in his heart, man amuses himself in a thousand different ways! Death is about, and he takes to the world's highroads with a song on his lips! Oh, I begin to think that man's soul has become hardened! Turn your horses around, charioteer; this is no time to wander through the flower-gardens. How can a sensible man, a man who knows what death is, seek pleasure in the hour of anguish?"

But the charioteer kept on driving toward the garden where the king had ordered him to take his son. There, at Suddhodana's command, Udayin, who was a son of the household priest and Siddhartha's friend since childhood, had assembled many beautiful maidens, skilled in the art of dancing and of song, and skillful also in the game of love.

10

THE chariot entered the wood. The young trees were in bloom, birds fluttered about joyously as though intoxicated by the light and atmosphere, and on the surface of the pools the lotuses had cupped their petals to drink in the cool air.

Siddhartha went unwillingly, like a young hermit, still new to his vows, who fears temptation and is taken to some celestial palace where lovely Apsarases are wont to dance. Filled with curiosity, the maidens rose and came forward as though to greet a betrothed. Their eyes were bright with admiration, and the hands they extended were like flowers. They all thought, "This is Kama himself come back to earth." But they did not speak nor even smile, so timid were they in his presence.

Udayin called to the boldest and the most beautiful, and he said to them:

"Why do you fail me to-day, you whom I have chosen from among many to captivate the prince, my friend? What makes you behave like shy, silent children? Your charm, your beauty, your boldness would win even a woman's heart, and you tremble

49

before a man! You mortify me. Come, wake up! Use your charms! Make him yield to love!"

One of the maidens spoke up:

"He frightens us, O master; his majestic splendor frightens us."

"Great as it is," replied Udayin, "it should not frighten you. For strange is the power of women. Let him remind you of all those who, in the past, have been at the mercy of a tender glance. Once upon a time the great hermit Vyasa, whom even the Gods were afraid to offend, was kicked by a courtesan called the Belle of Benares, and he was not displeased. The monk Manthalagotama, who was famous for his long penances, became an undertaker's assistant, in order to win the favor of the wanton Jangha, a woman of the very lowest caste. Santa artfully managed to seduce Rishyasringa, a learned man who had never known woman; and that most pious of all men, glorious Visvamitra, one day, in the forest, yielded to the importunities of the Apsaras Ghritaki. And I could name many more who succumbed to women like you, O lovely maidens! Come, do not be afraid of the king's son. Smile at him, and he will fall in love with you."

Udayin's words encouraged the maidens. Smiling, and with exquisite grace, they gradually formed a ring around the prince.

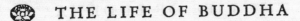

They used the most engaging wiles in order to approach Siddhartha, in order to brush past him or hold him and steal a caress. One pretended to stumble and clung to his girdle. Another drew near and mysteriously whispered in his ear, "Deign to hear my secret, O prince." Another feigned intoxication; she slowly unwound the blue veil that bound her breasts, then came and leaned against his shoulder. Another jumped down from the branch of a mango-tree and laughingly tried to stop him as he passed. Still another offered him a lotus-flower. And one sang: "Look, dear love, this tree is covered with blossoms, with blossoms whose perfume cloys the air; in the branches, rare birds trill their happy songs, as though in a golden cage. Listen to the bees, hovering over the flowers; they are roused and consumed by a burning ardor. Look at those creepers, warmly embracing the tree; the breeze ruffles them with a jealous hand. Over there, in that lovely glade, do you see the silver pool asleep? It is smiling, drowsily, like a maiden caressed by a bold moonbeam."

But the prince was not smiling; he was unhappy, for he was thinking on death.

He thought, "They do not know these maidens, that youth is fleeting, and that old age will come and strip them of their beauty! They are blind to the menace that is sickness, though it is already master of the world! They know nothing of death, of imperious death, of death that destroys everything! And that is why they can laugh, that is why they can play!"

Udayin tried to interrupt Siddhartha's thoughts. He said, "Why are you so discourteous to these maidens? Perhaps they do not interest you? What matter! Be kind to them, even at the cost of a few lies. Spare them the shame of being spurned. How can your beauty profit you if you are ungracious? You will be like a forest without flowers."

"What good are lies, what good is flattery?" replied the prince. "I would not deceive these women. Old age and death lie in wait for me. Do not try to tempt me, Udayin; do not ask me to join in any vulgar amusement. I have seen old age, I have seen sickness, I am certain of death; nothing now can give me peace of mind. And you would have me yield to love? Of what metal is that man made who knows of death and still seeks love? A cruel, implacable guard stands at his door, and he does not even weep!"

The sun was setting. The maidens had ceased their laughter; the prince had no eyes for their garlands and their jewels. They felt their charms were of no avail, and slowly they took the road back to the city.

The prince returned to the palace. King Suddhodana heard from Udayin that his son was shun-
ning all pleasure, and that night he found no sleep.

Gopa was waiting for the prince. He avoided her.
It made her anxious, and when she finally fell
asleep, she had a dream:

The whole earth shook; the tallest mountains
swayed; a savage wind blew, shattering and uprooting the trees. The sun, the moon and the stars had
fallen from the sky to the earth. She, Gopa, was
stripped of her clothes and of her ornaments; she
had lost her crown; she was naked. Her hair was
cut. The bridal bed was broken; the prince's robes
and the precious stones with which they were
embroidered were scattered about. Meteors sped
across the sky over a darkened city, and Meru, king
of the mountains, trembled.

Overcome with terror, Gopa awoke. She ran to
her husband.

"My lord, my lord," she cried, "what will happen? I have had a terrible dream! My eyes are full
of tears, and my heart is full of fear."

"Tell me your dream," the prince replied.

Gopa related all that she had seen in her sleep.
The prince smiled.

"Rejoice, Gopa," said he, "rejoice. You saw the
earth shake? Then one day the Gods themselves
shall bow before you. You saw the moon and the

sun fall from the sky? Then you shall soon defeat
evil, and you shall receive infinite praise. You saw
the trees uprooted? Then you shall find a way out
of the forest of desire. Your hair was cut short?
Then you shall free yourself from the net of passions that holds you captive. My robes and my
jewels were scattered about? Then I am on the
road to deliverance. Meteors were speeding across
the sky over a darkened city? Then to the ignorant
world, to the world that is blind, I shall bring the
light of wisdom, and those who have faith in my
words will know joy and felicity. Be happy, O
Gopa, drive away your melancholy; you will soon
be singularly honored. Sleep, Gopa, sleep; you have
dreamed a lovely dream."

11

SIDDHARTHA could no longer find peace. He strode through the halls of his palace like a lion stung by some poisoned dart. He was unhappy.

One day, there came to him a great longing for the open fields and the sight of green meadows. He left the palace, and as he strolled aimlessly through the country, he mused:

"It is indeed a pity that man, weak as he really is, and subject to sickness, with old age a certainty and death for a master, should, in his ignorance and pride, contemn the sick, the aged and the dead. If I should look with disgust upon some fellow-being who was sick or old or dead, I would be unjust, I would not be worthy of understanding the supreme law."

And as he pondered the misery of mankind, he lost the vain illusion of strength, of youth and of life. He knew no longer joy or grief, doubt or weariness, desire or love, hatred or scorn.

Suddenly, he saw a man approaching who looked like a beggar and who was visible to him alone.

"Tell me, who are you?" the prince asked him.

"Hero," said the monk, "through fear of birth and death, I became an itinerant monk. I seek deliverance. The world is at the mercy of destruction. I think not as other men; I shun pleasures; I know nothing of passion; I look for solitude. Sometimes I live at the foot of a tree; sometimes I live in the lonely mountains or sometimes in the forest. I own nothing; I expect nothing. I wander about, living on charity, and seeking only the highest good."

He spoke. Then he ascended into the sky and disappeared. A God had taken the form of a monk in order to arouse the prince.

Siddhartha was happy. He saw where his duty lay; he decided to leave the palace and become a monk.

He returned to the city. Near the gates he passed a young woman who bowed and said to him, "She who is your bride must know supreme blessedness, O noble prince." He heard her voice, and his soul was filled with peace: the thought had come to him of supreme blessedness, of beatitude, of nirvana.

He went to the king; he bowed and said to him:

"King, grant the request I have to make. Do not oppose it, for I am determined. I would leave the palace, I would walk in the path of deliverance. We must part, father."

The king was deeply moved. With tears in his voice, he said to his son:

"Son, give up this idea. You're still too young to consider a religious calling. Our thoughts in the springtime of life are wayward and changeable. Besides, it is a grave mistake to perform austere practises in our youth. Our senses are eager for new pleasures; our firmest resolutions are forgotten when we learn the cost in effort. The body wanders in the forest of desire, only our thoughts escape. Youth lacks experience. It is for me, rather, to embrace religion. The time has come for me to leave the palace. I abdicate, O my son. Reign in my stead. Be strong and courageous; your family needs you. And first know the joys of youth, then those of later years, before you betake yourself to the woods and become a hermit."

The prince answered:

"Promise me four things, O father, and I shall not leave your house and repair to the woods."

"What are they?" asked the king.

"Promise me that my life will not end in death, that sickness will not impair my health, that age will not follow my youth, that misfortune will not destroy my prosperity."

"You are asking too much," replied the king. "Give up this idea. It is not well to act on a foolish impulse."

Solemn as Meru mountain, the prince said to his father:

"If you can not promise me these four things, do not hold me back, O father. When some one is trying to escape from a burning house, we should not hinder him. The day comes, inevitably, when we must leave this world, but what merits is there in a forced separation? A voluntary separation is far better. Death would carry me out of the world before I had reached my goal, before I had satisfied my ardor. The world is a prison: would that I could free those beings who are prisoners of desire! The world is a deep pit wherein wander the ignorant and the blind: would that I could light the lamp of knowledge, would that I could remove the film that hides the light of wisdom! The world has raised the wrong banner, it has raised the banner of pride: would that I could pull it down, would that I could tear to pieces the banner of pride! The world is troubled, the world is in a turmoil, the world is a wheel of fire: would that I could, with the true law, bring peace to all men!"

With tears in his eyes, he returned to the palace. In the great hall Gopa's companions were laughing and singing. He paid no heed to them. Night came on, and they were silent.

They fell asleep. The prince looked at them.

Gone was their studied grace, gone the sparkle of their eyes. Their hair was dishevelled, their mouths gaped, their breasts were crushed, and their arms and legs were stiffly outstretched or clumsily twisted under them. And the prince cried:

"Dead! They are dead! I am standing in a grave-yard!"

And he left, and made his way toward the royal stables.

12

HE called his equerry, fleet Chandaka.

"Bring me my horse Kanthaka, at
once," said he. "I would be off, to find
eternal beatitude. The deep joy I feel, the indomi-
table strength that now sustains my will, the assur-
ance that I have a protector even though I am alone,
all these things tell me that I am about to attain my
goal. The hour has come; I am on the road to
deliverance."

Chandaka knew the king's orders, but he felt
some superior power urging him to disobey. He
went to fetch the horse.

Kanthaka was a magnificent animal; he was
strong and supple. Siddhartha stroked him quietly,
then said to him in a gentle voice:

"Many times, O noble beast, my father rode you
into battle and defeated his powerful enemies.
To-day, I go forth to seek supreme beatitude; lend
me your help, O Kanthaka! Companions in arms
or in pleasure are not hard to find, and we never
want for friends when we set out to acquire wealth;
but companions and friends desert us when it is
the path of holiness we would take. Yet of this

am I certain: he who helps another to do good or to do evil shares in that good or in that evil. Know then, O Kanthaka, that it is a virtuous impulse that moves me. Lend me your strength and your speed; the world's salvation and your own is at stake."

The prince had spoken to Kanthaka as he would have to a friend. He now eagerly climbed into the saddle, and he looked like the sun astride an autumn cloud.

The horse was careful to make no noise, for the night was clear. No one in the palace or in Kapilavastu was awakened. Heavy iron bars protected the gates of the city, an elephant could have raised them only with great difficulty, but, to allow the prince to pass, the gates opened silently, of their own accord.

Leaving his father, his son and his people, Siddhartha went forth from the city. He felt no regret, and in a steady voice, he cried:

"Until I shall have seen the end of life and of death, I shall not return to the city of Kapila."

13

KANTHAKA bravely carried him a great distance. When the sun finally peered between the eyelids of night, the most noble of men saw that he was near a wood where dwelt many pious hermits. Deer were asleep under the trees, and birds fluttered about fearlessly. Siddhartha felt rested, and he thought he need go no further. He dismounted and gently stroked his horse. There was happiness in his glance and in his voice as he said to Chandaka:

"Truly, a horse has the strength and swiftness of a God. And you, dear friend, by bearing me company, have proved to me how great is your affection and your courage. It was a noble deed and pleases me. Those who, like yourself, can combine energy and devotion are indeed rare. You have shown that you are my friend, and you expect no reward from me! Yet it is usually a selfish interest that brings men together. I assure you, you have made me very happy. Take the horse now and return to the city. I have found the forest I was seeking."

The hero took off his jewels and handed them to Chandaka.

"Take this necklace," said he, "and go to my father. Tell him to believe in me and not give way to his grief. If I enter a hermitage, it is not because I am wanting in affection for my friends or because my enemies provoke my anger; nor is it because I seek a place among the Gods. Mine is a worthier reason: I will destroy old age and death. Therefore, do not grieve, Chanda, and do not let my father be unhappy. I left my home to be rid of unhappiness. Unhappiness is born of desire; that man is to be pitied who is a slave to his passions. When a man dies, there are always heirs to his fortune, but heirs to his virtues are rarely found, are never found. If my father says to you, 'He left for the forest before the appointed time,' you will answer that life is so uncertain that the practise of virtue is never untimely. Say this to the king, O my friend, and do your best to make him forget me. Tell him that I possess neither virtue nor merit; for a man without virtue is never loved, and he who is never loved is never mourned."

With tears in his eyes, Chandaka replied:

"Oh, how they will weep, those who love you! You are young, you are beautiful, the palace of the Gods should be your home; yet you would live in the woods and sleep on the coarse grass? I knew of

63

your cruel resolve; I should not have gone to fetch
Kanthaka; but a supernatural power urged me,
deceived me, and I brought him to you. How
could I have done such a thing of my own will?
Sorrow will now find its way into Kapilavastu. O
prince, your father loves you dearly, do not forsake him! And Mahaprajapati? What has she not
done for you! She is your foster-mother; do not be
ungrateful! And is there not still another woman
who loves you? Do not abandon faithful Gopa!
Raise your son with her help, and one day he will
bring you glory!"

He wept bitterly. The hero was silent. Chanda
continued:

"You are going to leave your family for ever!
Oh, if you must cause them grief, spare me, at
least, the anguish of imparting the sad news!
What would the king say to me if he saw me return
without you? What would your mother say to me?
What would Gopa say? And when I appear before
your father, you ask me to deny your merit and
your virtue! How can I do that, my lord? I can
not lie. And even if I should decide to lie, who
would believe me? Who can be made to believe that
the moon has fiery beams?"

He seized the hero's hand.

"Do not forsake us! Come **back, oh, come back!**"

Siddhartha still remained silent. Finally, he said in a solemn voice:

"We must part, Chanda. There comes a time when people who are bound by the closest ties must go their own ways. If, out of love for my family, I were not to leave, death would still separate us, in spite of everything. What am I now to my mother? What is she to me? Birds that sleep in the same tree at night scatter to the four winds at the first flush of dawn; clouds that some puff of wind has brought together by another puff of wind are again dispersed. I can no longer live in a world that is but a dream. We must part, my friend. Tell the people of Kapilavastu that I have done nothing worthy of blame, tell them to forget their affection for me; and tell them also that they will see me again, soon, the conquerer of old age and death, unless I should fail miserably and die."

Kanthaka was licking his feet. The hero gently stroked his horse and spoke to him as though to a friend:

"Do not weep. You have shown that you are a noble animal. Be patient. The time is near when your toil will be rewarded."

Then he took a sword that Chandaka was holding. The hilt was of gold and was studded with jewels; the blade was sharp. With one blow he cut off his hair, then tossed the sword into the air where it glistened like a new star. The Gods caught it and held it in great reverence.

But the hero was still wearing his gorgeous robe. He wanted a plain one, one suitable to a hermit. Whereupon a hunter appeared, wearing a coarse garment made of a reddish material. Siddhartha said to him:

"Your peaceful robe is like those worn by hermits; it offers a strange contrast to your savage bow. Give me your clothes and take mine in exchange. They will suit you better."

"Thanks to these clothes," said the hunter, "I can deceive the beasts in the forests. They do not fear me, and I can kill them at close range. But if you have need of them, my lord, I shall willingly give them to you and take yours in exchange.

Siddhartha joyfully donned the coarse, reddish-colored clothes belonging to the hunter, and the hunter reverently accepted the hero's robe, then he disappeared into the sky. Siddhartha realized that the Gods themselves had wished to present him with his hermit's robe, and he rejoiced. Chandaka was filled with wonder.

Arrayed in his reddish-colored robes, the saintly hero set out on the path to the hermitage. He was like the king of the mountains wrapped in clouds at dusk.

And Chandaka, with a heavy heart, took the road back to Kapilavastu.

14

GOPA had awakened in the deep of night. A strange uneasiness possessed her. She called to her beloved, Prince Siddhartha, but there was no answer. She rose. She ran through the halls of the palace; he was nowhere to be found. She became frightened. Her maidens were asleep. A cry escaped her lips:

"Oh, wicked, wicked! You have betrayed me! You have allowed my beloved to escape!"

The maidens awoke. They searched every room. There was no longer any doubt: the prince had left the palace. Gopa rolled on the ground; she tore her hair, and her face bore the marks of her deep despair.

"He once told me that he would go away, far away, he, the king of men! But I never thought the cruel parting would come so soon. Oh, where are you, my well-beloved? Where are you? I can not forget you, I, who am forlorn, so forlorn! Where are you? Where are you? You are so beautiful! Your beauty is unrivalled among men. Your eyes sparkle. You are good, and you are beloved, my well-beloved! Were you not happy? Oh, my dear, my beloved, where have you gone?"

Her companions tried in vain to console her.

"Hereafter, I will drink only to quench my thirst, I will eat only to still my hunger. I will sleep on the bare ground, for crown I will wear a hermit's braid, no more sweet-scented baths will I take, I will mortify my flesh. The gardens are bare of flowers and of fruit; the faded garlands are heavy with dust. The palace is deserted. No longer will it ring with the happy songs of yesterday."

Mahaprajapati learned from one of her maidens of Siddhartha's flight. She went to Gopa. The two women wept in each other's arms.

King Suddhodana heard the lamentation. He asked the reason. A servant went to inquire and returned with this answer:

"My lord, the prince can not be found anywhere in the palace."

"Close the gates of the city," cried the king, "and search for my son in the streets, in the gardens, in the houses."

He was obeyed, but the prince was nowhere to be found. The king broke down.

"My son, my only child!" he sobbed, and fell into a swoon. He was soon brought to, and he ordered:

"That horsemen be dispatched in all directions, and that they bring me back my son!"

69

In the meanwhile, Chandaka and the horse Kanthaka were slowly returning from the hermitage. As they approached the city, they both hung their heads in dejection. Some horsemen espied them.

"It is Chandaka! It is Kanthaka!" they cried, and they galloped their horses. They saw that Chandaka was carrying the prince's jewels. They asked, anxiously:

"Was the prince murdered?"

"No, no," Chandaka quickly replied. "He entrusted me with his jewels that I might return them to his family. He has donned a hermit's robe, and he has entered a forest where dwell some holy men."

"Do you think," said the horsemen, "that if we went to him, we could persuade him to return with us?"

"Your words would be futile. He is obdurate. He said, 'I shall not return to Kapilavastu until I have conquered old age and death.' And what he has said, he will do."

Chandaka followed the horsemen to the palace. The king summoned him at once.

"My son! My son! Where has he gone, Chandaka?"

The equerry told him what the prince had done. The king grieved, yet he could not help admiring his son's greatness.

Gopa and Mahaprajapati entered; they had heard of Chandaka's return. They questioned him, and they learned of Siddhartha's high resolve.

"O you who were my joy," said Gopa through her tears, "you whose voice was so sweet, you who had such strength and such grace, such knowledge and such virtue! When you spoke to me, I thought I was listening to some lovely song, and when I leaned over you, I inhaled the perfume of all the flowers. Now I am far away from you, and I weep. What shall become of me, now, for he is gone, he who was my guide? I shall know poverty, for I have lost my treasure. He was my eyes; I can no longer see the light; I am blind. Oh, when will he return, he who was my joy?"

Mahaprajapati saw the jewels Chandaka had brought back with him. She stood looking at them a great while. She was weeping. Then, taking the jewels, she left the palace.

Still weeping, she walked through the garden until she came to a pool. Once again, she looked at the jewels, then threw them into the water.

Kanthaka had returned to the stables. The other horses were happy at his return and neighed in a friendly manner. But he did not hear them; he did not see them. He was very sad. He whinnied pitifully once or twice, and, suddenly, fell dead.

15

SIDDHARTHA had entered the hermitage where holy Arata Kalama taught the doctrine of renunciation to a great number of disciples. Whenever he appeared, they all admired him; wherever he went, there shone a marvellous light. The monks listened with joy when he spoke, for his voice was sweet and powerful, and he was persuasive. One day, Arata Kalama said to him:

"You understand the law as well as I understand it; all that I know, you know. Hereafter, if you wish, we will share the work; we will both teach the disciples."

The hero asked himself: "Is the law that Arata teaches the true law? Does it lead to deliverance?"

He thought: "Arata and his disciples lead lives of great austerity. They refuse food prepared by man; they will eat only fruit, leaves and roots; they will drink only water. They are more abstemious than the birds that peck at minute seeds, than the deer that nibble at the grass, than the serpents that inhale the breeze. When they sleep, it is under a canopy of branches; the heat of the sun scorches them; they expose their bodies to the bitter winds; they bruise their feet and their knees on the stones of the highway. To them, virtue comes only with suffering. And they think they are happy, for they believe that by practising perfect austerity, they will earn the right to ascend to the sky! Yes, they will ascend to the sky! But the human race will continue to suffer old age and death! To lead a life of austerity and be indifferent to the constant evil of birth and death is simply to add suffering to suffering. Men tremble in the presence of death, yet they do their utmost to be reborn; they keep plunging deeper and deeper into the very pit they fear. If it is an act of piety to mortify the flesh, then it must be impious to indulge in sensuality, but mortifications in this world are followed by gratifications in the next, and thus the reward of piety is impiety. If, to be sanctified, it is enough simply to be abstemious, then the deer would be saints, and those men also would be saints who have lost caste, for to them an evil fate has made pleasure unattainable. But, it will be said, it is the intention to suffer that develops religious virtue. The intention! We can intend to gratify our senses as well as we can intend to suffer, and if the intention to gratify our senses is worth nothing, why should the intention to suffer be of any value?"

Thus did he ponder in the hermitage of Arata Kalama. He saw the vanity of the doctrine that the master was teaching, and he said to him:

"I will not teach your doctrine, Arata. Who knows it will not find deliverance. I shall leave your hermitage, and I shall seek the rule to which we must submit before we can have done with suffering."

And the hero set out for the country of Magadha, and there, alone and absorbed in meditation, he dwelt on the slope of a mountain, near the city of Rajagriha.

O NE morning, the hero took his alms-bowl and entered the city of Rajagriha. The people who passed him on the road admired his beauty and his noble bearing. "What is this man?" they wondered. "He is like a God, like Sakra or Brahma himself." Presently, it was noised abroad that a marvellous being was wandering through the city, begging. Every one wanted to see the hero; they followed him about, and women rushed to the windows as he passed by. But he gravely pursued his way, while over the city a strange light appeared.

A man ran to inform the king that a God, no less, was begging in the streets of the city. King Vimbasara went out on the terrace of the palace; he saw the hero. His splendor dazzled him. He sent him alms, and he gave orders to have him followed, in order to discover his retreat. Thus did the king learn that the magnificent beggar lived on the slope of the mountain, near the city.

The following day, Vimbasara drove out of the city and came to the mountain. He left his chariot, and, quite alone, walked toward a tree in whose shade the hero was seated. The king paused near the tree, and, speechless with wonder, reverently gazed at the beggar.

Then, bowing humbly, he said:

"I have seen you and great is my joy! Do not remain here on the lonely mountain-side; sleep no longer on the hard ground. You are beautiful, you are resplendent with youth; come to the city. I will give you a palace, and all your desires shall be gratified."

"My lord," replied the hero, in a gentle voice, "my lord, may you live many years! Desires mean nothing to me. I lead the life of a hermit; I know peace."

"You are young," said the king, "you are beautiful, you are ardent; be rich. You shall have the loveliest maidens in my kingdom to serve you. Do not go away; stay and be my companion."

"I have given up great riches," said the hero.

"I will give you half my kingdom."

"I have given up the most beautiful of kingdoms."

"Here you may gratify all your desires."

"I know the vanity of all desire. Desires are like poison; wise men despise them. I have thrown them away as one would throw away a wisp of dry straw. Desires are as perishable as the fruit on a

tree, they are as wayward as the clouds in the
sky, they are as treacherous as the rain, they are
as changeable as the wind! Suffering is born of desire, for no man has ever gratified all his desires. But
they that seek wisdom, they that ponder the true
faith, they are the ones that find peace. Who drinks
salt water increases his thirst; who flees from desire
finds his thirst appeased. I no longer know desire.
I seek the true law."

The king said:

"Great is your wisdom, O beggar! Which is your
country? Where is your father? Where is your
mother? Which is your caste? Speak."

"Perhaps you have heard of the city of Kapilavastu, O king? A prosperous city it is. The king,
Suddhodana, is my father. I left him in order to
wander and beg."

The king replied:

"Good fortune attend you! I am happy now
that I have seen you. Between your family and
mine there is a friendship of long standing. Be
gracious to me, and when you have gained en-
lightenment, deign to teach me, O master."

He bowed three times, then returned to Rajagriha.

The hero heard that there lived near Rajagriha a
famous hermit named Rudraka, son of Rama. This
hermit had many disciples whom he instructed in

77

the law. The hero went to listen to his teachings, but like Arata Kalama, Rudraka knew nothing of the true law, and the hero did not tarry.

Presently he came to the banks of the Nairanjana. Five of Rudraka's disciples: Kaundinya, Asvajit, Vashpa, Mahanaman and Bhadrika, had joined him.

17

THE clear waters of the Nairanjana flowed through a rich and fertile land. Little villages drowsed in the shade of magnificent trees, and great meadows stretched away into the distance. The hero thought, "How pleasant it is here; what an inviting spot in which to meditate! Perhaps, here, I shall find the path to wisdom. Here I shall dwell."

He became deeply absorbed in contemplation. He was so engrossed with his thoughts that he stopped breathing, and, one day, he fell into a swoon. The Gods, who were watching him from the sky, thought he was dead, and they cried:

"Is he dead, this child of the Sakyas? Has he died and left the world to its suffering?"

Maya, the hero's mother, lived among the Gods. She heard their cries and plaints, and she feared for the life of her son. Attended by a host of Apsarases, she descended to the banks of the Nairanjana, and when she saw Siddhartha, so stiff, so inert, she wept.

She said:

79

"When you were born in the garden, I was assured, O my son, that you would behold the truth. And later, Asita predicted that you would set the world free. But they were all lies, these predictions. You did not win fame by any royal conquest, you did not attain supreme knowledge! You died, pitifully and alone. Who will help you, O my son? Who will bring you back to life? For ten moons I carried you in my womb, O my jewel, and now I can only grieve."

She scattered flowers over the body of her son, whereupon he stirred and spoke to her in a gentle voice:

"Have no fear, mother; your labor was not in vain; Asita told you no lie. Even if the earth crumble into dust, even if Meru sink below the waters, even if the stars fall like rain upon the earth, I shall not die. I, alone, of all men, will survive the world's ruin! Do not weep, mother! The time is approaching when I shall attain supreme knowledge."

Maya smiled at her son's words; three times she bowed, then ascended to the sky, to the music of celestial lutes.

For six years, the hero remained on the banks of the river and meditated. He never sought shelter from the wind, from the sun or from the rain; he allowed the gadflies, the mosquitoes and the serpents

to sting him. He was oblivious to the boys and girls, the shepherds and woodcutters, who jeered at him as they passed by and who sometimes threw dust or mud at him. He hardly ate: a fruit and a few grains of rice or of sesame composed his fare. He became very thin; his bones showed prominently. But under his gaunt forehead, his dilated eyes shone like stars.

And yet true knowledge did not come to him. He felt he was becoming very weak, and he realized that if he wasted away, he would never reach the goal he had set for himself. So he decided to take more nourishment.

There was a village called Uruvilva near the spot where Siddhartha spent long hours in meditation. The head man of this village had ten daughters. They revered the hero, and they brought him grain and fruit by way of alms. He rarely touched these gifts, but, one day, the girls noticed that he had eaten all they had offered him. The next day, they came with a large dish full of boiled rice, and he emptied that. The following day, each one brought a different delicacy, and the hero ate them all. He began to gain flesh, and, presently, he started going to the village to beg his food. The inhabitants vied with one another in giving him alms, and, before long, he had regained his strength and his beauty.

But the five disciples who had joined him said to each other:

"His austerities did not lead him into the path of true knowledge, and now he has ceased to practice them. He takes abundant nourishment; he seeks comfort. He no longer thinks of doing holy deeds. How can he, now, attain true knowledge? We considered him a wise man, but we were mistaken: he is a madman and a fool."

And they left him and went to Benares.

18

THE hero's clothes had become threadbare in the six years he had been wearing them, and he thought:

"It would be well if I had some new clothes; otherwise I shall have to go naked, and that would be immodest."

Now, Sujata, the most devout of the ten young girls who had been bringing him food, had a slave who had just died. She had wrapped the body in a shroud made of a reddish material and had had it carried to the cemetery. The dead slave was lying in the dust. The hero saw the body as he passed; he went over to it and removed the shroud.

It was very dusty, and the hero had no water in which to wash it. Sakra, from the sky, saw his perplexity. Coming down to earth he struck the ground, and a pool appeared before the eyes of the Saint.

"Good," said he, "here is water, but I still need a wash-stone."

Sakra made a stone and set it down on the edge of the pool.

"Man of virtue," said the God, "give me the shroud; I shall wash it for you."

83

"No, no," replied the Saint. "I know the duties of a monk; I myself shall wash the shroud."

When it was clean, he bathed. Now, Mara, the Evil One, had been watching for him for some time. He suddenly raised the banks of the pool, making them very steep. The Saint was unable to climb out of the water. Fortunately, there was a tall tree growing near the pool, and the Saint addressed a prayer to the Goddess who lived in it.

"O Goddess, may a branch of this tree bend over me!"

A branch immediately bent over the pool. The Saint caught hold of it and pulled himself out of the water. Then he went and sat down under the tree, and he began to sew on the shroud and make a new garment for himself.

Night came on. He fell asleep, and he had five dreams.

First, he saw himself lying in a large bed that was the whole earth; under his head, there was a cushion which was the Himalaya; his right hand rested on the western sea, his left hand on the eastern sea, and his feet touched the southern sea.

Then he saw a reed coming out of his navel, and the reed grew so fast that it soon reached the sky.

Then he saw worms crawling up his legs and completely covering them.

Then he saw birds flying toward him from all

84

points of the horizon, and when the birds were near his head, they seemed to be of gold.

Finally, he saw himself at the foot of a mountain of filth and excrement; he climbed the mountain; he reached the summit; he descended, and neither the filth nor the excrement had defiled him.

He awoke, and from these dreams he knew that the day had come when, having attained supreme knowledge, he would become a Buddha.

He rose and set out for the village of Uruvilva, to beg.

Sujata had just finished milking eight wonderful cows that she owned. The milk they gave was rich, oily and of a delicate savor. She added honey and rice flour to it, then set the mixture to boil in a new pot, on a new stove. Huge bubbles began to form and kept floating off to the right, without the liquid rising or spilling a single drop. The stove did not even smoke. Sujata was astonished, and she said to Purna, her servant:

"Purna, the Gods are favoring us to-day. Go and see if the holy man is approaching the house."

Purna, from the doorstep, saw the hero walking toward Sujatà's house. He was diffusing a brilliant light, a golden light. Purna was dazzled. She ran back to her mistress.

"Mistress, he is coming! He is coming! And your eyes will be blinded by his splendor!"

"Let him come! Oh, let him come!" cried Sujata. "It is for him that I have prepared this wonderful milk."

She poured the milk mixed with honey and flour into a golden bowl, and she awaited the hero.

He entered. The house was lighted up by his presence. Sujata, to do him honor, bowed seven times. He sat down. Sujata kneeled and bathea his feet in sweet-scented water; then she offered him the golden bowl full of milk mixed with rice flour and honey. He thought:

"The Buddhas of old, it is said, had their last meal served to them in a golden bowl, before attaining supreme knowledge. Since Sujata offers me this milk and honey in a golden bowl, the time has come for me to be a Buddha."

Then he asked the young girl:

"Sister, what must I do with this golden bowl?"

"It belongs to you," she replied.

"I have no use for such a bowl," said he.

"Then do as you please with it," said Sujata. "It would be contemptible of me to offer the food and not offer the bowl."

He left, carrying the bowl in his hands, and he walked to the banks of the river. He bathed; he ate. When the bowl was empty, he threw it into the water, and he said:

"If I am to become Buddha this very day, may

the bowl go upstream; if not, may it go with the current."

The bowl floated out to the middle of the river, then rapidly started upstream. It disappeared in a whirlpool, and the hero heard the muffled ring as it landed, in the subterranean world, among those other bowls the former Buddhas had emptied and thrown away.

The hero sauntered along the banks of the river. Night slowly descended. The flowers wearily closed their petals; a sweet fragrance rose from the fields and gardens; the birds timidly rehearsed their even-songs.

It was then the hero walked toward the tree of knowledge.

The road was sprinkled with gold-dust; rare palms, covered with precious stones, lined the way. He skirted the edge of a pool whose blessed waters exhaled an intoxicating perfume. White, yellow, blue and red lotuses spread their massive petals over the surface, and the air rang with the clear songs of the swans. Near the pool, under the palms, Apsarases were dancing, while in the sky the Gods were admiring the hero.

He approached the tree. On the side of the road, he saw Svastika, the reaper.

"They are tender, these grasses you are mowing, Svastika. Give me some grass; I want to cover

the seat I shall occupy when I attain supreme
knowledge. They are green, these grasses you are
mowing, Svastika. Give me some grass, and you will
know the law some day, for I shall teach it to you,
and you may teach it to others."

The reaper gave the Saint eight handfuls of grass.

There stood the tree of knowledge. The hero
went to the east of it and bowed seven times. He
threw the handfuls of grass on the ground, and,
suddenly, a great seat appeared. The soft grass covered it like a carpet.

The hero sat down, his head and shoulders erect,
his face turned to the east. Then he said in a solemn
voice:

"Even if my skin should parch, even if my hand
should wither, even if my bones should crumble
into dust, until I have attained supreme knowledge
I shall not move from this seat."

And he crossed his legs.

THE light emanating from the hero's body reached even to those realms where Mara, the Evil One, reigned supreme. It dazzled Mara, and he seemed to hear a voice saying:

"The hero who has renounced royalty, the son of Suddhodana, is now seated under the tree of knowledge. He is concentrating his mind, he is making the supreme effort, and soon he will bring to all creatures the help which they need. The road he will have taken, others will take. Once set free, he will set others free. Once he has found peace, he will bring peace to others. He will enter nirvana, and he will cause others to enter. He will find wisdom and happiness, and he will give them to others. Because of him, the city of the Gods will be crowded; because of him, the city of the Evil One will be deserted. And you, Mara, a commander without an army, a king without subjects, will not know where to take refuge."

Mara was filled with apprehension. He tried to sleep, but his slumber was disturbed by terrible dreams. He awoke and summoned his servants and his soldiers. When they saw him, they became

alarmed, and Sarthavaha, one of his sons, said to him:

"Father, you look pale and unhappy; your heart beats fast and your limbs tremble. What have you heard? What have you seen? Speak."

"Son," replied Mara, "the days of my pride are over. I heard a voice crying in the light, and it told me that the son of the Sakyas was seated under the tree of knowledge. And I had horrible dreams. A black cloud of dust settled over my palace. My gardens were bare of leaves, of flowers and of fruit. My ponds had dried up, and my swans and peacocks had their wings clipped. And I felt alone, amid this desolation. You had all deserted me. My queen was beating her breast and tearing her hair, as though haunted by remorse. My daughters were crying out in their anguish, and you, my son, were bowing before this man who meditated under the tree of knowledge! I wanted to fight my enemy, but I could not draw my sword from the scabbard. All my subjects fled in horror. Impenetrable darkness closed in upon me, and I heard my palace crashing to the ground."

Sarthavaha said:

"Father, it is disheartening to lose a battle. If you have seen these omens, bide your time, and do not run the chance of being ingloriously defeated."

But Mara, at the sight of the legions that surrounded him, felt his courage return. He said to his son:

"To the man of energy, a battle can end only in victory. We are brave; we will surely win. What strength can this man have? He is alone. I shall advance against him with a vast army, and I shall strike him down at the foot of the tree."

"Mere numbers do not make the strength of an army," said Sarthavaha. "The sun can outshine a myriad of glowworms. If wisdom is the source of his power, a single hero can defeat countless soldiers."

But Mara paid no heed. He ordered the army to advance at once, and Sarthavaha thought:

"He who is insane with pride will never recover."

Mara's army was a fearful sight. It bristled with pikes, with arrows and with swords; many carried enormous battle-axes and heavy clubs. The soldiers were black, blue, yellow, red, and their faces were terrifying. Their eyes were cruel flames; their mouths spewed blood. Some had the ears of a goat, others the ears of a pig or of an elephant. Many had bodies shaped like a jug. One had the paws of a tiger, the hump of a camel and the head of a donkey; another had a lion's mane, a rhinoceros' horn and a monkey's tail. There were many with two, four and five heads, and others with ten, twelve and twenty arms. In place of ornaments, they wore jawbones, skulls and withered human fingers. And shaking their hairy heads, they advanced with hideous laughter and savage cries:

"I can shoot a hundred arrows at one time; I shall seize the body of the monk." "My hand can crumple up the sun, the moon and the stars; how easy it will be to crush this man and his tree." "My eyes are full of poison: they would dry up the sea; I shall look at him, and he will burn to a cinder."

Sarthavaha kept to himself. A few friends had gathered around him, and they were saying:

"Fools! You think he is mad because he meditates; you think he is craven because he is calm. It is you who are madmen, it is you who are cowards. You do not know his power; because of his great wisdom he will defeat you all. Were your numbers as infinite as the grains of sand on the banks of the Ganges, you would not disturb a single hair of his head. And you believe you can kill him! Oh, turn back! Do not try to harm him; bow before him in reverence. His reign has come. The jackals howl in the forests when the lion is away, but when the lion roars, the jackals scamper off in terror. Fools, fools! You shout with pride while the master is silent, but when the lion speaks you will take to your heels."

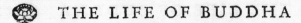

The army listened with contempt to these words of wisdom spoken by Sarthavaha and his friends. It kept advancing.

Before attacking the hero, Mara sought to frighten him. He roused against him the fury of the winds. Fierce gales rushed toward him from the horizon, uprooting trees, devastating villages, shaking mountains, but the hero never moved; not a single fold of his robe was disturbed.

The Evil One summoned the rains. They fell with great violence, submerging cities and scarring the surface of the earth, but the hero never moved; not a single thread of his robe was wet.

The Evil One made blazing rocks and hurled them at the hero. They sped through the air but changed when they came near the tree, and fell, not as rocks, but flowers.

Mara then commanded his army to loose their arrows at his enemy, but the arrows, also, turned into flowers. The army rushed at the hero, but the light he diffused acted as a shield to protect him; swords were shivered, battle-axes were dented by it, and whenever a weapon fell to the ground, it, too, at once changed into a flower.

And, suddenly, filled with terror at the sight of these prodigies, the soldiers of the Evil One fled.

And Mara wrung his hands in anguish, and he cried:

"What have I done that this man should defeat me? For they are not a few, those whose desires I have granted! I have often been kind and generous! Those cowards who are fleeing could bear witness to that."

The troops that were still within hearing answered:

"Yes, you have been kind and generous. We will bear witness to that."

"And he, what proof has he given of his generosity?" continued Mara. "What sacrifices has he made? Who will bear witness to his kindness?"

Whereupon a voice came out of the earth, and it said:

"I will bear witness to his generosity."

Mara was struck dumb with astonishment. The voice continued:

"Yes, I, the Earth, I, the mother of all beings, will bear witness to his generosity. A hundred times, a thousand times, in the course of his previous existences, his hands, his eyes, his head, his whole body have been at the service of others. And in the course of this existence, which will be the last, he will destroy old age, sickness and death. As he excels you in strength, Mara, even so does he surpass you in generosity."

And the Evil One saw a woman of great beauty emerge from the earth, up to her waist. She bowed before the hero, and clasping her hands, she said:

"O most holy of men, I bear witness to your generosity."

Then she disappeared.

And Mara, the Evil One, wept because he had been defeated.

95

ॐ

BY sunset the army of the Evil One had fled.
Nothing had disturbed the hero's meditation, and, in the first watch of the night,
he arrived at the knowledge of all that had trans-
pired in previous existences. In the second watch,
he learned the present state of all beings. In the
third, he understood the chain of causes and effects.

He now clearly saw all creatures being con-
tinually reborn, and, whether of high or of low
caste, in the path of virtue or of evil, he saw them
going through the round of existences, at the
mercy of their actions. And the hero thought:

"How miserable is this world that is born, grows
old and dies, then is reborn only to grow old and
die again! And man knows no way out!"

And in profound meditation, he said to himself:

"What is the cause of old age and death? There
is old age and death because there is birth. Old age
and death are due to birth. What is the cause of

birth? There is birth because there is existence. Birth is due to existence. What is the cause of existence? There is existence because there are ties. Existence is due to ties. What is the cause of ties? There are ties because there is desire. Ties are due to desire. What is the cause of desire? There is desire because there is sensation. Desire is due to sensation. What is the cause of sensation? There is sensation because there is contact. Sensation is due to contact. What is the cause of contact? There is contact because there are six senses. Contact is due to the six senses. What is the cause of the six senses? There are six senses because there is name and form. The six senses are due to name and form. What is the cause of name and form? There is name and form because there is perception. Name and form are due to perception. What is the cause of perception? There is perception because there is impression. Perception is due to impression. What is the cause of impression? There is impression because there is ignorance. Impression is due to ignorance."

And he thought:

"Thus does ignorance lie at the root of death, of old age, of suffering, of despair. To suppress ignorance is to suppress impression. To suppress impression is to suppress perception. To suppress perception is to suppress name and form. To suppress

97

name and form is to suppress the six senses. To suppress the six senses is to suppress contact. To suppress contact is to suppress sensation. To suppress sensation is to suppress desire. To suppress desire is to suppress ties. To suppress ties is to suppress existence. To suppress existence is to suppress birth. To suppress birth is to suppress old age and death. To exist is to suffer. Desire leads from birth to rebirth, from suffering to further suffering. By stifling desire, we prevent birth, we prevent suffering. By leading a life of holiness, desire is stifled, and we cease to endure birth and suffering."

When dawn appeared, this most noble of men was a Buddha. He exclaimed:

"I have had numerous births. In vain have I sought the builder of the house. Oh, the torment of perpetual rebirth! But I have seen you at last, O builder of the house. You no longer build the house. The rafters are broken; the old walls are down. The ancient mountain crumbles; the mind attains to nirvana; birth is no more for desire is no more."

Twelve times the earth shook; the world was like a great flower. The Gods sang:

"He has come, he who brings light into the world; he has come, he who protects the world! Long blinded, the eye of the world has opened, and the eye of the world is dazzled by the light.

O conquerer, you will give all beings that which they hunger after. Guided by the sublime light of the law, all creatures will reach the shores of deliverance. You hold the lamp; go now and dispel the darkness!"

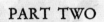

PART TWO

THE Buddha never moved. He remained under the tree, his legs crossed. He was filled with bliss at having attained perfect knowledge. He thought, "I have found deliverance." One whole week he remained under the tree of knowledge, without moving.

The second week he went on a long journey; he travelled through all the worlds.

The third week he again remained under the tree of knowledge, and he never once blinked his eyes.

The fourth week he went on a short journey, from the eastern sea to the western sea.

It was then that Mara, whom defeat had left inconsolable, went to the Buddha and spoke these evil words:

"Blessed One, why do you tarry, you who know the path to deliverance? Blow out the lamp, quench the flame; enter nirvana, O Blessed One; the hour has come."

But the Blessed One answered:

"No, Mara, I shall not quench the flame, I shall

not enter nirvana. I must first gain many disciples, and they, in turn, must win others over to my law. By word and by deed I must silence my adversaries. No, Mara, I shall not enter nirvana until the Buddha is glorified throughout the world, until his beneficent law is recognized."

Mara left him. He was crestfallen, and he seemed to hear divine voices mocking him.

"You have been defeated, Mara," they were saying, "and you stand wrapped in thought, like an old heron. You are powerless, Mara, like an aged elephant stuck fast in a swamp. You thought you were a hero, and you are weaker than a sick man abandoned in a forest. Of what avail were your insolent words? They were as futile as the chattering of crows."

He picked up a piece of dead wood, and began drawing figures in the sand. His three daughters, Rati, Arati and Trishna, saw him. They were taken aback at the sight of his grief.

"Father, why are you so melancholy?" asked Rati.

"I have been defeated by a saintly man," replied Mara. "He is proof against my strength and my cunning."

"Father," said Trishna, "we are beautiful; we have seductive ways."

"We shall go to this man," continued Arati; "we

shall bind him with the chains of love, and we shall bring him to you, humbled and craven."

They went to the Buddha, and they sang:

"Spring is here, friend, the loveliest of the seasons. The trees are in blossom; we must be merry. Your eyes are beautiful, they shine with a lovely light, and you bear the marks of omnipotence. Look at us: we were made to give pleasure and happiness to both men and Gods. Rise and join us, friend; make the most of your shining youth; dismiss all solemn thoughts from your mind. Look at our hair, see how soft it is; flowers lend their fragrance to its silkiness. See our eyes wherein slumbers the sweetness of love. See our warm lips, like fruit ripened in the sun. See our firm, rounded breasts. We glide with the stately grace of swans; we know songs that charm and please, and when we dance, hearts beat faster and pulses throb. Come, friend, do not spurn us; he is foolish, indeed, who would throw away a treasure. Look at us, dear Lord; we are your slaves."

But the Blessed One was unmoved by the song. He frowned at the young girls, and they turned into hags.

In despair they returned to their father.

"Father," cried Rati, "see what he has done to our youth and our beauty."

"Love will never hurt him," said Trishna, "for he was able to resist our charms."

"Oh," sighed Arati, "how cruelly he has punished us."

"Father," implored Trishna, "cure us of this hideous old age."

"Give us back our youth," cried Rati.

"Give us back our beauty," cried Arati.

"My poor daughters," replied Mara, "I grieve for you. Yes, he has defeated love; he is beyond my power, and I am sad. You plead with me to give you back your youth and your beauty, but how can I? The Buddha alone can undo what the Buddha has done. Return to him; admit that you were blame-worthy; tell him that you are repentant, and per-haps he will give you back your charms."

They implored the Buddha.

"Blessed One," said they, "forgive us our offense. Our eyes were blind to the light, and we were foolish. Forgive us!"

"Yes, you were foolish," replied the Blessed One; "you were trying to destroy a mountain with your finger-nails, you were trying to bite through iron with your teeth. But you acknowledge your of-fense; that already is a sign of wisdom. O maidens, I forgive you."

And the three daughters of the Evil One left his presence, more beautiful than ever before.

The fifth week the Blessed One remained un-der the tree. But, suddenly, there blew a bitter

wind, and a cold rain fell. Then Mucilinda, the serpent-king, said to himself: "The Blessed One must not suffer from the rain or from the cold." He left his home. Seven times he coiled himself around the Buddha, and he spread his hood above the Buddha's head to shelter him. And thus the Buddha suffered not at all during this period of bad weather.

The sixth week he went to a fig-tree where goatherds often forgathered. There, some Gods awaited him, and they humbly bowed as he approached. He said.

"Meekness is sweet to him who knows the law; kindness is sweet to him who can see; meekness is sweet to all creatures; kindness is sweet to all creatures. Blessed is he who has not a desire in the world; blessed is he who has conquered sin; blessed is he who has escaped the torture of the senses; blessed is he who no longer thirsts for existence!"

The seventh week he remained under the tree of knowledge.

Two brothers, Trapusha and Bhallika, were returning to the northern countries. They were merchants and had five hundred chariots in their train. As they came near the tree, the chariots stopped. In vain did the drivers try to encourage or goad the beasts that drew them; they could not advance a step. The wheels kept sinking in the mud up to the hubs. Trapusha and Bhallika became alarmed, but a God appeared who reassured them and said:

"Walk a little way, O merchants, and you will find one to whom you should do homage."

Trapusha and Bhallika saw the Blessed One. His face was radiant.

"Is it the God of some river or the God of the mountain?" they wondered. "Could it be Brahma himself?"

But upon looking at his garments, they thought:

"It must be some monk. Perhaps he would like something to eat."

Trapusha and Bhallika went to the chariot that carried the provisions. They found flour and honey cakes, and they brought them to the Buddha.

"Take them, saintly man," they said, offering him the cakes, "take them and be gracious to us."

The Blessed One had no bowl in which to receive alms. He did not know what to do. The Gods, who were watching at the four quarters of the earth, saw his perplexity, and they quickly brought him bowls made of gold. But the Blessed One said to himself:

"Truly, it would be unseemly for a monk to receive alms in a golden bowl."

And he refused the golden bowls. The Gods then brought him silver bowls, which he also refused.

He likewise refused emerald bowls, and he would only accept bowls made of stone.

He then received the cakes the merchants offered him. When he had finished eating, he said:

"The blessing of the Gods be with you, merchants! Prosper and be happy!"

Trapusha and Bhallika bowed, and they heard a God say to them:

"He who is before you has arrived at supreme knowledge. This was his first meal since he found the path to deliverance, and to you fell the signal honor of offering it to him. He will now go through the world and teach the true law."

Trapusha and Bhallika rejoiced, and they were the first to profess their faith in the Buddha and in the law.

ς

THE Buddha began to wonder how he would propagate the knowledge. He said to himself:

"I have discovered a profound truth. It was difficult to perceive; it will be difficult to understand; only the wise will grasp it. In a world full of confusion, men lead restless lives, yet men enjoy living in a world full of confusion. How then can they understand the chain of causes and effects? How can they understand the law? They will never be able to stifle their desires; they will never break away from earthly pleasures; they will never enter nirvana. If I preach the doctrine, I shall not be understood. Perhaps no one will even listen to me. What is the use of revealing to mankind the truth I had to fight to win? Truth stays hidden from those controlled by desire and hatred. Truth is hard to find; it remains ever a mystery. The vulgar mind will never grasp it. He will never know truth whose mind is lost in darkness, who is a prey to earthly desires."

And the Blessed One was not inclined to preach the doctrine.

Then Brahma, by virtue of his supreme intelligence, knew of the doubts that beset the Blessed One. He became frightened. "The world is lost," he said to himself, "the world is undone, if the Perfect One, the Holy One, the Buddha, now stands aloof, if he does not go among men to preach the doctrine and propagate the knowledge."

And he left the sky. It took him less time to reach the earth than it takes a strong man to bend or stretch his arm, and he appeared before the Blessed One. To show his deep reverence, he uncovered one shoulder, then kneeling, he raised his folded hands to the Blessed One and said:

"Deign to teach the knowledge, O Master, deign to teach the knowledge, O Blessed One. There are men of great purity in the world, men whom no filth has ever defiled, but, if they are not instructed in the knowledge, how will they find salvation? They must be saved, these men; oh, save them! They will listen to you; they will be your disciples."

Thus spoke Brahma. The Blessed One remained silent. Brahma continued:

"Till now an evil law has prevailed in the world. It has led men into sin. It behooves you to destroy it. O Man of Wisdom, open for us the gates of eternity; tell us what you have found, O Savior! You are he who has climbed the mountain, you

stand on the rocky summit, and you survey mankind from afar. Have pity, O Savior; think of the
unhappy peoples who suffer the anguish of birth
and of old age. Go, conquering hero, go! Travel
through the world, be the light and the guide.
Speak, teach; there will be many to understand
your word."

And the Blessed One answered:

"Profound is the law that I have established; it
is subtile and hard to understand; it lies beyond
ordinary reasoning. The world will scoff at it; only
a few wise men perhaps will grasp the meaning and
decide to accept it. If I set out, if I speak and am
not understood, I risk an ignominious defeat. I
shall stay here, Brahma; men are the sport of ignorance."

But Brahma spoke again:

"You have attained sublime wisdom; the rays of
your light reach even into space, yet you are indifferent, O Sun! No, such conduct is unworthy of
you; your silence is reprehensible; you must speak.
Rise up! Beat the drums, sound the gong! Let the
law blaze like a burning torch, or like refreshing
rain, let it fall upon the parched earth. Deliver
those who are tormented by evil; bring peace to
those consumed by a vicious fire! You, who are like
a star among men, you alone can destroy birth and

death. See, I fall at your feet and implore you, in the name of all the Gods!"

Then the Blessed One thought:

"Among the blue and white lotuses that flower in a pool, there are some that stay under water, others that rise to the surface, and still others that grow so tall that their petals are not even wet. And in the world I see good men and evil men; some have sharp minds and others are dull; some are noble, others ignoble; some will understand me, others will not; but I shall take pity on them all. I shall consider the lotus that opens under water as well as the lotus that flaunts its great beauty."

And he said to Brahma:

"May the gates of eternity be open to all! May all who have ears hear the word and believe! I was thinking of the weariness in store for me and fearing the effort would come to nothing, but my pity outweighs these considerations. I rise, O Brahma, and I shall preach the law to all creatures."

₃

THE Blessed One wondered who was worthy of being the first to hear the word of salvation.

"Where is there a man of virtue, intelligence and energy, to whom I can teach the law?" he asked himself. "His heart must be innocent of hatred, his mind must be tranquil, and he must not keep the knowledge to himself as if it were some dark secret."

He thought of Rudraka, son of Rama. He remembered that he had been free from hatred and had tried to lead a life of virtue, and that he was not the sort of man who would make a secret of the knowledge. He decided to teach him the law, and this question arose in his mind: "Where is Rudraka, now?" Then he learned that Rudraka, son of Rama, had been dead seven days, and he said:

"It is a great pity that Rudraka, son of Rama, should have died without hearing the law. He would have understood it, and he, in turn, could have taught it."

He thought of Arata Kalama. He remembered his clear intellect and his virtuous life, and he decided that Arata Kalama would be glad to propagate the knowledge. And this question arose in his mind: "Where is Arata Kalama now?" Then he learned that Arata Kalama had been dead three days, and he said:

"Arata Kalama died without hearing the law; great is Arata Kalama's loss."

He thought again, and he remembered Rudraka's five disciples who had once joined him. They were virtuous; they were energetic; they would certainly understand the law. The Blessed One knew, by virtue of his intelligence, that Rudraka's five disciples were living in the Deer Park at Benares. So he set out for Bernares.

At Mount Gaya he met a monk named Upaka. At the sight of the Blessed One, Upaka uttered a cry of admiration.

"How beautiful you are!" he exclaimed. "Your face is radiant. Fruit that has ripened in the sun has less bloom. Yours is the beauty of a clear autumn. My Lord, may I ask who your master was?"

"I had no master," answered the Blessed One. "There is no one like me. I alone am wise, calm, incorruptible."

"What a great master you must be!" said Upaka.

"Yes, I am the only master in this world; my equal can not be found on earth or in the sky."

"Where are you going?" asked Upaka.

"I am going to Benares," said the Blessed One, "and there I shall light the lamp that will bring light into the world, a light that will dazzle even the eyes of the blind. I am going to Benares, and there I shall beat the drums that will awaken mankind, the drums that will sound even in the ears of the deaf. I am going to Benares, and there I shall teach the law."

He continued on his way, and he came to the banks of the Ganges. The river was high, and the Blessed One looked for a boatman to take him across. He found one and said to him:

"Friend, will you take me across the river?"

"Certainly," replied the boatman, "but first pay me for the trip."

"I have no money," said the Blessed One.

And he flew through the air to the opposite bank.

The boatman was heart-broken. He cried, "I did not take him across the river, he who was such a saintly man! Oh, woe is me!" And he rolled on the ground in his great distress.

THE Blessed One entered the great city of Benares. He wandered through the streets, asking for alms; he ate the food that was given him, then he went to the Deer Park where he knew he would find Rudraka's former disciples.

The five disciples saw him in the distance. They thought they recognized him, and they said to each other:

"Do we not know this man, walking toward us? Is he not the one whose austerities, formerly, used to astonish us, and who, one day, revolted against the severe self-discipline he had been observing? If his mortifications did not show him the way to supreme knowledge then, how can his thoughts profit us to-day when he is swayed by greed and cowardice? Let us not go and meet him, or rise when he approaches; let us not relieve him of his cloak or of his alms-bowl; let us not even offer him a seat. We will say to him, 'All the seats here are taken.' And we will give him nothing to eat or drink."

Thus did they decide. But the Blessed One kept

drawing nearer, and the closer he came the more uncomfortable they felt. They were seized with a great desire to rise from their seats. They were like birds frantically trying to escape from a cage under which a fire has been kindled. They were restless; they seemed to be ill. Finally, they broke their resolution. They rose as one man; they ran to the Blessed One, and they greeted him. One took his alms-bowl, another his cloak; a third offered him a seat. They brought him water to bathe his feet, and with one voice they cried:

"Welcome, friend, welcome. Take a seat in our midst."

The Blessed One sat down and bathed his feet. Then he said to the five hermits:

"Do not address me as friend, O monks. I am the Saint, the Perfect One, the supreme Buddha. Open your ears, O monks; the path is discovered that leads to deliverance. I will show you the path; I will teach you the law. Listen well, and you will learn the sacred truth."

But they answered:

"Formerly, in spite of your austere practises, you did not arrive at perfect knowledge, so how could you have attained it, now that you lead a life of self-indulgence?"

"O monks," replied the Blessed One, "I do not lead a life of self-indulgence; I have renounced none of the blessings to which I aspired. I am the Saint, the Perfect One, the supreme Buddha. Open your ears, O monks; the path is discovered that leads to deliverance. I will show you the path; I will teach you the law. Listen well, and you will learn the sacred truth."

He added, "O monks, will you admit that I have never before addressed you in this manner?"

"We admit it, Master."

"I say unto you: I am the Saint, the Perfect One, the supreme Buddha. Open your ears, O monks; the path is discovered that leads to deliverance. Listen well."

And the five monks listened as he spoke.

"There are two extremes that he must avoid who would lead a life governed by his intelligence. Some devote themselves to pleasure; their lives are a constant round of dissipations; they seek only to gratify their senses. Such beings are contemptible; their conduct is ignoble and futile; it is unworthy of him who would acquire intelligence. Others devote themselves to self-mortification; they deprive themselves of everything; their conduct is gloomy and futile; it is unworthy of him who would acquire intelligence. From these two extremes, O monks, the Perfect One stands aloof. He has discovered the middle path, the path that opens the eyes and opens the mind, the path that leads to

rest, to knowledge, to nirvana. This sacred path, O monks, has eight branches: right faith, right resolve, right speech, right action, right living, right effort, right thought, right meditation. This, O monks, is the middle path, the path that I, the Perfect One, discovered, the path that leads to rest, to knowledge, to nirvana."

All five held their breath, the better to hear him. He paused a moment, then continued:

"O monks, I will tell you the truth about suffering. Suffering is birth, suffering is old age, suffering is sickness, suffering is death. You are bound to that which you hate: suffering; you are separated from that which you love: suffering; you do not obtain that which you desire: suffering. To cling to bodies, to sensations, to forms, to impressions, to perceptions: suffering, suffering, suffering. O monks, I will tell you the truth about the origin of suffering. The thirst for existence leads from rebirth to rebirth; lust and pleasure follow. Power alone can satisfy lust. The thirst for power, the thirst for pleasure, the thirst for existence; there, O monks, is the origin of suffering. O monks, I will tell you the truth about the suppression of suffering. Quench your thirst by annihilating desire. Drive away desire. Forgo desire. Free yourselves of desire. Be ignorant of desire. O monks, I will tell you the truth about the path that leads to the extinc-

tion of suffering. It is the sacred path, the noble eight-fold path: right faith, right resolve, right speech, right action, right living, right effort, right thought, right meditation. O monks, you know the sacred truth about suffering; no one before me had discovered it; my eyes opened, and suffering was revealed to me. I understood the truth about suffering; you, O monks, must now understand it. O monks, you know the sacred truth about the origin of suffering; no one before me had discovered it; my eyes opened, and the origin of suffering was revealed to me. I understood the truth about the origin of suffering; you, O monks, must now understand it. O monks, you know the sacred truth about the suppression of suffering; no one before me had discovered it; my eyes opened, and the suppression of suffering was revealed to me. I understood the truth about the suppression of suffering; you, O monks, must now understand it. O monks, you know the sacred truth about the path that leads to the extinction of suffering; no one before me had discovered it; my eyes opened, and the path that leads to the extinction of suffering was revealed to me. I understood the truth about the path that leads to the extinction of suffering; you must now understand it, O monks."

The five disciples listened with rapture to the words of the Blessed One. He spoke again:

"O monks, as long as I did not have a complete understanding of these four truths, I knew that neither in this world nor in the world of the Gods, in Mara's world nor in Brahma's world I knew that among all beings, men, Gods, hermits or brahmans, I had not attained the supreme rank of Buddha. But, O monks, now that I have a complete understanding of these four truths, I know that in this world as in the world of the Gods, in Mara's world and in Brahma's world, I know that among all beings, men, Gods, hermits or brahmans, I have attained the supreme rank of Buddha. I am for ever set free: for me there will be no new birth."

Thus spoke the Blessed One, and the five monks joyfully acclaimed him and glorified him.

KAUNDINYA was the first of the five monks to approach the Blessed One. He said:

"I have listened, O Master, and if you consider me worthy, I will be your disciple."

"Did you understand me, Kaundinya?" the Blessed One asked.

"I have faith in the Buddha and the Buddha I would follow," said Kaundinya. "I would follow him who has the knowledge, who knows the worlds, who is a Saint; I would follow him who tames all beings as one tames wild bulls, whose words are heeded by both Gods and men; I would follow him who is the supreme Buddha. I have faith in the law and the law I would follow. The Blessed One has expounded it; it has been clearly set forth; it leads to salvation, and the wise must acknowledge its beneficent power. According to your precepts would I live, according to your saintly precepts, to your precepts that the wise shall praise."

"You have understood, Kaundinya," said the Blessed One. "Come nearer. Well preached is the law. Lead a saintly life, and have done with suffering."

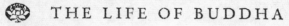

Then Vashpa came to the Buddha to profess his faith, and he was followed by Bhadrika, Mahanaman and Asvajit. And presently there were six saints in the world.

The Blessed One was still in the Deer Park when a young man named Yasas arrived. Yasas was the son of a wealthy merchant of Benares. He had been leading a worldly existence, but he had learned the vanity of such things, and he was now seeking the sacred peace of the woods. The Blessed One saw Yasas; he spoke to him, and Yasas announced that he was ready to walk in the path of holiness.

The father of Yasas came to the Deer Park to look for his son. He wanted to discourage him, to make him turn aside from the path of holiness. But he heard the Buddha speak; his words impressed him, and he believed in him. The mother and the wife of Yasas also professed their belief in the truth of the law, but while Yasas joined the monks, his father, his mother and his wife returned to their home in Benares.

Four friends of Yasas, Vimala, Subahu, Purnajit and Gavampati, were amused at the step he had taken. They said:

"Let us go to the Deer Park and look for Yasas. We shall convince him of his mistake, and he will return with us."

Upon entering the wood, they found the Buddha instructing his disciples. He was saying:

"There was once a hermit who dwelt in a ravine far up in the mountains. He lived miserably and alone. His clothes were made out of bark; he drank only water, and he ate nothing but roots and wild fruit. His sole companion was a hare. This hare could speak like a human being, and he liked to talk to the hermit. He derived great benefit from his teachings, and he strove earnestly to attain wisdom. Now, one year, there was a terrible drought: the mountain springs dried up, and the trees failed to flower or bear fruit. The hermit could no longer find food or water; he became weary of his mountain retreat, and, one day, he cast aside his hermit's robe. The hare saw him and said, 'Friend, what are you doing?' 'You can see for yourself,' replied the hermit. 'I have no further use for this robe.' 'What!' exclaimed the hare, 'are you going to leave the ravine?' 'Yes, I shall go among people. I shall receive alms, and they will give me food, not just roots and fruit.' At these words the hare became frightened; he was like a child abandoned by its father, and he cried, 'Do not go, friend! Do not leave me alone! Besides, many are ruined who go to live in cities! The solitary life of the forest is alone praiseworthy.' But the hermit was determined: he had decided to go, he would go. Then the hare said to him: 'You would leave the mountains? Then leave! But grant me this favor: wait a day longer, just one day. Stay here to-day, to-morrow you may do as you please.' The hermit thought, 'Hares are good foragers; they often have a store of provisions hidden away. To-morrow this one may bring me something to eat.' So he promised not to leave until the following day, and the hare scampered off joyously. The hermit was one of those who held Agni in great reverence, and he was careful always to keep a fire burning in the ravine. 'I have no food,' he said to himself, 'but at least I can keep warm until the hare returns.' At dawn the following day, the hare reappeared, empty-handed. The hermit's face betrayed his disappointment. The hare bowed to him and said, 'We animals have neither sense nor judgment; forgive me, worthy hermit, if I have done wrong.' And he suddenly leaped into the flames. 'What are you doing?' cried the hermit. He sprang to the fire and rescued the hare. Then the hare said to him, 'I would not have you fail in your duty; I would not have you leave this retreat. There is no longer any food to be had. I have given my body to the flames; take it, friend; feed upon my flesh. and stay in the ravine.' The hermit was deeply moved. He replied, 'I shall not take the road to the city; I shall remain here, even if I must die of starvation.' The hare was happy; he looked up at the sky and murmured this prayer: 'Indra, I have always loved the life of solitude. Deign to hear me, and cause the rain to fall.' Indra heard the prayer. The rain fell in torrents, and presently the hermit and his friend found all the food they wanted in the ravine."

After a moment of silence, the Blessed One added:

"At that time, O monks, the hare was I. As for the hermit, he was one of the evil-minded young men who have just entered the Deer Park. Yes, you were he, Vimala!"

He rose from his seat.

"Just as I kept you from following the evil path when I was a hare living in the ravine, Vimala, so shall I show you the way to holiness, now that I have become the supreme Buddha, and your eyes will see, your ears will hear. Why, you are already blushing with shame at having tried to prevent your best friend from finding salvation!"

Vimala fell at the feet of the Blessed One. He professed his faith in him, and he was received among the disciples. Then Subahu, Purnajit and Gavampati also decided to accept the sacred word.

Each day the number of disciples increased, and soon the master had sixty monks ready to propagate the knowledge. He said to them:

"O disciples, I am free of all bonds, human and divine. And you, too, are now free. So start on your way, O disciples, go, out of pity for the world, for the world's happiness, go. It is to you that Gods and men will owe their welfare and their joy. Set out on the road, singly and alone. And teach, O disciples, teach the glorious law, the law glorious in the beginning, glorious in the middle, glorious in the end; teach the spirit of the law; teach the letter of the law; to all who hear, proclaim the perfect, the pure, the saintly life. There are some who are not blinded by the dust of the earth, but they will not find salvation if they do not hear the law proclaimed. So go, O disciples, go and teach them the law."

The disciples scattered, and the Blessed One took the road to Uruvilva.

THE LIFE OF BUDDHA

6

THE Blessed One had been walking a long while. He was weary. Coming to a small wood, he entered and sat down at the foot of a tree. He was about to fall asleep when a band of thirty young men entered the wood. He watched them.

From their words and behavior, it was evident that they were looking for some one. They finally addressed the Buddha.

"Did you see a woman pass by?" they asked.

"No. Who are you?"

"We are musicians. We wander from city to city. We have often played before kings, for our skill is greatly admired. We brought a young girl along with us to-day, for our pleasure, but while we were sleeping, over there, by the side of the road, she stole all that she could take with her and fled. It is she we are seeking."

"Which is better," the Buddha asked: "that you go in search of this woman, or that you go in search of yourselves?"

The musicians laughed at the Master.

"Play your lute," he then said to the one who was laughing the loudest.

The musician played. He was skillful; it was easy to believe that kings delighted in his playing. When he had finished the Master said:

"Give me your lute."

And he played. The musicians listened with amazement. They never knew such sweet notes could be plucked from a lute. Even the wind was silent, and the Goddesses of the wood left their verdant retreats, the better to hear him.

The Blessed One stopped playing.

"Master," said the musicians, "we thought we were skilled in our art, and we are ignorant of its first principles. Deign to teach us all you know."

The Blessed One replied, "You suspect, now, that your knowledge of music is superficial, yet you once thought you had mastered the art. And so you think you know yourselves, but your knowledge is only superficial. You earnestly ask me to teach you all I know about music, yet you laugh when I tell you to go in search of yourselves!"

The musicians were no longer laughing.

"We understand you, Master," they cried, "we understand you! We shall go in search of ourselves."

"It is well," said the Buddha. "You will learn

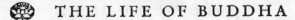

the law from me. Then, like King Padmaka, who sacrificed his body to save his people, you will give your intelligence to save mankind."

And the musicians listened with rapt attention while he told the story of King Padmaka.

"There once reigned in Benares a just and powerful king named Padmaka. Now, a strange epidemic suddenly swept through the city. Those who were stricken turned completely yellow, and, even in the sunshine, they shivered with cold. The king took pity on his subjects, and he tried to find some way to cure them. He consulted the most famous physicians; he distributed medicines, and he himself helped to nurse the sick. But it was hopeless; the epidemic continued to rage. Padmaka grieved. One day, an old physician came to him and said, 'My lord, I know a remedy that will cure the inhabitants of Benares.' 'What is it?' asked the king. 'It is a large fish named Rohita. Have him caught, and give a piece, no matter how small, to all who are sick, and the epidemic will disappear.' The king thanked the old physician; he ordered the fish Rohita to be sought in the seas and in the rivers, but nowhere could it be found. The king was in despair. Sometimes in the morning or in the evening, he would hear plaintive voices crying outside the palace walls, 'We are suffering, O king; save us!' And he would weep bitterly. Finally, he thought: 'What

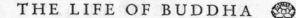

good is wealth or royalty, what good is life, if I can not succor those who are racked with pain?' He summoned his eldest son, and he said to him, 'My son, I leave you my fortune and my kingdom.' Then he ascended to the terrace of the palace; he offered perfume and flowers to the Gods, and he cried, 'Gladly do I sacrifice a life that I consider useless. May the sacrifice benefit those who are afflicted! May I become the fish Rohita and be found in the river that flows through the city!' He threw himself from the terrace and immediately reappeared in the river as the fish Rohita. He was caught; he was still alive when they cut him into pieces to distribute among the sick, but he never felt the knives, and he quivered with love for all creatures. The epidemic soon disappeared, and over the city of Benares, a celestial choir sang: 'It was Padmaka, the holy king, who saved you! Rejoice!' And they all did honor to Padmaka's memory."

The musicians listened to the Master, and they promised to follow him, to receive the knowledge.

In Uruvilva, the Blessed One found the three Kasyapa brothers. These virtuous brahmans had a thousand disciples. For some time they had been bothered by a dangerous serpent that kept disturbing their sacrifices, and they brought their troubles to the Buddha. The Buddha smiled; he watched for the serpent and ordered it, in the future, to leave them in peace. The serpent obeyed, and the sacrifices were no longer interrupted.

The Kasyapas asked the Buddha to stay with them a few days. He consented. He astounded his hosts by performing innumerable prodigies, and presently they all decided to accept the law. The eldest of the Kasyapas alone refused to follow the Buddha. He thought:

"True, this monk is very powerful; he performs great prodigies, but he is not my equal in holiness."

The Blessed One read Kasyapa's thoughts. He said to him:

"You think you are a very holy man, Kasyapa, and you are not even in the path that leads to holiness."

Kasyapa was astonished that the Buddha should have guessed his secret thoughts. The Blessed One added:

"You do not even know how to find the path that leads to holiness. Hearken to my words, Kasyapa, if you would dispel the darkness in which you live."

Kasyapa thought for a moment; then he fell at the feet of the Blessed One, and he said:

"Instruct me, O Master! Let me walk no longer in the night!"

Then the Blessed One ascended a mountain, and

he addressed the Kasyapa brothers and their disciples.

"O monks," said he, "everything in the world is aflame. The eye is aflame; all that it sees is aflame; all that we behold in the world is aflame. Why? Because the fire of love and of hatred is not extinguished. You are blinded by the flames of this fire, and you suffer the torment of birth and of old age, of death and of misery. O monks, everything in the world is aflame! Understand me, and for you the fire will be extinguished; your eyes will no longer be blinded by the flames, and you will no longer enjoy the blazing spectacle in which you delight to-day. Understand me, and you will know that there is an end to birth, you will know that to this earth we need never return."

T

THE Blessed One remembered that King Vimbasara had once expressed a desire to know the law, and he resolved to go to Rajagriha. He set out with the eldest Kasyapa and a few of his new disciples, and he went to live in a wood, near the city.

Vimbasara soon learned of the arrival of the monks. He decided to pay them a visit. Accompanied by a host of retainers, he went to the wood. He recognized the Master, and he exclaimed:

"You did not forget my wish, O Blessed One; great is my gratitude and my reverence."

He prostrated himself, and when the Master bade him rise, he stood at a distance, to show his respect.

But in the crowd there were some who knew Kasyapa, and who considered him a very saintly man. They had never seen the Buddha before, and they were astonished that the king should do him such honor.

He has surely made a mistake," said one brahman; "he should have prostrated himself before Kasyapa."

"Yes," said another, "Kasyapa is a great master."

"The king has made a strange blunder," a third added; "he has mistaken the pupil for the master."

They were speaking in whispers, yet the Blessed One heard them, for what could escape his notice? He said to Kasyapa:

"Who persuaded you to leave your hermitage, O man of Uruvilva? Who made you admit your weakness? Answer, Kasyapa; how did you come to leave your familiar retreat?"

Kasyapa understood what the Master had in mind. He replied:

"I know now where my former austerities were tending; I know the vanity of all that I once taught. My discourse was evil, and I began to hate the life I was leading."

As he said these words, he fell at the Master's feet, and he added:

"I am your devoted pupil. Let me lay my head upon your feet! You are the Master; it is you who command. I am your pupil, your servant. You will I heed and you will I obey."

Seven times he prostrated himself, and the crowd exclaimed in admiration:

"Mighty is he who has convinced Kasyapa of his ignorance! Kasyapa thought he was the greatest of teachers, and now see him bow before another! Oh, mighty is he who is Kasyapa's master!"

Then the Blessed One spoke to them of the four great truths. When he had finished, King Vimbasara approached him, and, in front of them all, boldly uttered these words:

"I believe in the Buddha, I believe in the law, I believe in the community of the saints."

The Blessed One gave the king leave to sit beside him, and the king spoke again:

"In my lifetime I have had five great hopes: I hoped that some day I would be king; I hoped that some day the Buddha would come into my kingdom; I hoped that some day my gaze would rest upon his countenance; I hoped that some day he would teach me the law; I hoped that some day I would profess my faith in him. To-day, all these hopes are realized. I believe in you, my Lord, I believe in the law, I believe in the community of the saints."

He rose.

"O Master, deign to take your meal at my palace, to-morrow."

The Master consented. The king left; he knew great happiness.

Many of those who had accompanied the king now followed his example, and professed their faith in the Buddha, in the law and in the community of the saints.

The next day, the inhabitants of Rajagriha left

their homes and went to the wood; they were eager to see the Blessed One. They all admired him, and they praised his power and his glory.

The time came for him to go to the king's palace, but the road was so crowded with spectators that it was impossible to advance a step. Suddenly, a young brahman appeared before the Master. No one knew whence he came. He said:

"The gentle Master is among gentle folk; he brings deliverance. He who shines like gold has come to Rajagriha."

He had a pleasant voice. He beckoned to the crowd to make way, and they obeyed without a thought of resisting. And he sang:

"The Master has dispelled the darkness; night will never be reborn; he who knows the supreme law has come to Rajagriha."

"Where does he come from, this young brahman with the clear, sweet voice?" the people wondered.

He continued to sing:

"He is here, he who is omniscient, the gentle Master, the sublime Buddha. He is supreme in the world; I am happy to serve him. Not to serve the ignorant, but humbly to serve the wise and to venerate those who are noble: is there in the world a holier joy? To live in a land of peace, to do many good works, to seek the triumph of righteousness:

138

is there in the world a holier joy? To have skill and knowledge, to love acts of generosity, to walk in the path of justice: is there in the world a holier joy?"

The young brahman managed to make a way through the crowd, and he led the Master to the palace of King Vimbasara. Then, his work done, he rose from the earth, and upon attaining the highest reaches of the sky, vanished into the light. And the people of Rajagriha knew that a God had deemed it an honor to serve the Buddha and exalt his grandeur.

Vimbasara received the Blessed One with great reverence. At the end of the meal, he said to him:

"I rejoice at your presence, my Lord. I must see you often, and often hear the sacred word from your lips. You must now accept a gift from me. Nearer the city than that forest where you dwell, there is a pleasant wood, known as the Bamboo Grove. It is vast; you and your disciples can live there in comfort. I give you the Bamboo Grove, my Lord, and if you will accept it, I shall feel that you have done me a great service."

The Buddha smiled with pleasure. A golden basin was brought, filled with sweet-scented water. The king took the basin and poured the water over the Master's hands. And he said:

"As this water pours from my hands into your

hands, my Lord, so may the Bamboo Grove pass from my hands into your hands, my Lord."

The earth trembled: the law now had soil in which to take root. And that same day, the Master and his disciples went to live in the Bamboo Grove.

8

TWO young brahmans, Sariputra and Maudgalyayana, were living at that time in the city of Rajagriha. They were intimate friends and were both pupils of the hermit Sanjaya. To each other they had made this promise: "Whichever one of us first obtains deliverance from death will immediately tell the other."

One day, Sariputra saw Asvajit collecting alms in the streets of Rajagriha. He was struck by his pleasant countenance, his noble and modest demeanor, his quiet and dignified bearing. He said to himself:

"Verily, there is a monk who, already in this world, has found the sure path to saintliness. I must go up to him; I must ask him who his master is and what law he obeys."

But then he thought:

"This is not the proper time to question him. He is collecting alms; I must not disturb him. I shall follow him, and when he is satisfied with the offerings he has received, I shall approach and speak to him."

The venerable Asvajit presently stopped asking for alms. Then Sariputra went up to him and greeted him in a friendly manner. Asvajit returned Sariputra's greeting.

"Friend," said Sariputra, "serene is your countenance, clear and radiant your glance. Who persuaded you to renounce the world? Who is your master? What law do you obey?"

"Friend," replied Asvajit, "that great monk, the son of the Sakyas, is my master."

"What does your master say, friend; what does he teach?"

"Friend, I left the world but recently; I have known the law only a short time; I can not expound it at great length, but I can give you briefly the spirit of it."

"Do, friend," cried Sariputra. "Say little or say much, as you please; but give me the spirit of the law. To me the spirit only matters."

The venerable Asvajit spoke this one sentence:

"The Perfect One teaches the cause, the Perfect One teaches the ends."

Sariputra rejoiced at these words. It was as if the truth had been revealed to him. "All that is born has an end," he thought. He thanked Asvajit, and, filled with hope, he went to find Maudgalyayana.

"Friend," said Maudgalyayana when he saw

Sariputra, "friend, how serene is your countenance! How clear and radiant your glance! Have you obtained deliverance from death?"

"Yes, friend. Near Rajagriha, there is a master who teaches deliverance from death."

Sariputra told of his encounter, and the two friends decided to go to the Blessed One. Their master, Sanjaya, tried to dissuade them.

"Stay with me," said he; "I will give you a position of eminence among my disciples. You will become masters and be my equals."

"Why should we want to be your equals? Why should we disseminate ignorance? We know now what your teaching is worth. It would make us masters of ignorance."

Sanjaya continued to urge them; suddenly, warm blood gushed from his mouth. The two friends drew back in horror.

They left and went to the Buddha.

"Here," said the Master as he saw them approach, "here are the two men who will be the foremost among my disciples."

And he joyfully welcomed them to the community.

9

THE number of believers was constantly increasing, and King Vimbasara gave repeated evidence to the Master of his faith and friendship. He often invited him to the palace and offered him a seat at his table, and at such times he would order the city to have a festive appearance. The streets were carpeted with flowers, and the houses decorated with banners. The sweetest perfumes filled the air, and the inhabitants dressed in their brightest clothes. The king himself would come forward to greet the Blessed One and would shade him from the sun with his golden parasol.

Many young nobles put all their faith in the law taught by the Blessed One. They wanted to become saints; they abandoned family and fortune, and the Bamboo Grove was soon filled with devout disciples.

But there were many in Rajagriha who were disturbed to see the great number of converts the Buddha was making, and they went about the city, voicing their anger.

"Why has he settled in our midst, this son of the Sakyas?" they would ask. "Were there not enough monks already, preaching to us about virtue? And they did not lure our young men away like this master. Why, even our children are leaving us. Because of this son of the Sakyas, how many women are widows! Because of this son of the Sakyas, how many families are childless! Evil will befall the kingdom, now that this monk has settled in our midst!"

The Master soon had a great many enemies among the inhabitants of the city. Whenever they met his disciples, they would taunt them or make sarcastic remarks.

"The great monk came to the city of Rajagriha and conquered the Bamboo Grove; will he now conquer the entire kingdom of Magadha?" said one as he went by.

"The great monk came to the city of Rajagriha and took Sanjaya's disciples away from him; who will he lure away to-day?" said another.

"A plague would be less harmful than this great monk," said a third; "it would kill fewer children."

"And it would leave fewer widows," a woman sighed.

The disciples made no reply. But they felt the anger of the populace growing, and they told the

145

Master of the evil words they had heard.
"Do not let it disturb you, O disciples," replied the Buddha. "They will soon stop. To those who follow you with jeers and insults, speak quiet, gentle words. Say to them, 'It is because they know the truth, the real truth, that the heroes convince, that the perfect ones convert. Who dares offend the Buddha, the Saint who converts by the power of truth?' Then they will be silent, and in a few days, when you wander through the city, you will meet only with respect and praise."

It happened as the Buddha had said. The evil voices were silenced, and every one in Rajagriha did honor to the Master's disciples.

10

KING Suddhodana heard that his son had attained supreme knowledge and that he was living at Rajagriha, in the Bamboo Grove. He had a great desire to see him again, and he sent a messenger to him, with these words: "Your father, King Suddhodana, longs to see you, O Master."

When the messenger arrived at the Bamboo Grove, he found the Master addressing his disciples.

"There is a forest clinging to the slope of a mountain, and at the foot of the mountain, a wide, deep pool. Wild beasts live on the banks of this pool. A man appears who would harm these beasts, who would make them suffer, who would let them die. He closes up the good path that leads away from the pool, the path that is safe to travel, and he opens up a treacherous path that ends in a dreadful swamp. The beasts are now in danger; one by one, they will perish. But let a man appear who, on the contrary, seeks the welfare of these wild beasts, who seeks their comfort, their prosperity. He will destroy the treacherous path that ends in a swamp, and he will open up a safe path that leads to the peaceful mountain top. Then the beasts will no longer be in danger; they will thrive and multiply. Now understand what I have told you, O disciples. Like these beasts on the banks of the wide, deep pool, man lives near the pleasures of the world. He who would do him harm, who would make him suffer, who would let him die, is Mara, the Evil One. The swamp wherein all beings perish is pleasure, desire, ignorance. He who seeks the welfare, the comfort, the prosperity of all is the Perfect One, the Saint, the blessed Buddha. It was I, O disciples, who opened up the safe path; it was I who destroyed the treacherous path. You will not go to the swamp; you will climb the mountain and reach the bright summit. All that a master can do who pities his disciples and who seeks their welfare, I have done for you, O my disciples."

The messenger listened in a transport of delight. Then he fell at the Master's feet and said:

"Receive me among your disciples, O Blessed One."

The Master extended his hands and said:

"Come, O monk."

The messenger stood up, and, suddenly, his clothes, of their own accord, took the shape and color of a monk's robe. He forgot everything, and the message that Suddhodana had entrusted to him was never delivered.

The king became weary of waiting for his return. Each day, the desire to see his son became more intense, and he sent another messenger to the Bamboo Grove. But for this man's return he also waited in vain. Nine times he sent messengers to the Blessed One, and nine times the messengers, upon hearing the sacred word, decided to remain and become monks.

Suddhodana finally summoned Udayin.

"Udayin," said he, "as you know, of the nine messengers who set out for the Bamboo Grove, not one has returned, not one has sent me word how my message was received. I do not know if they spoke to my son, if they even saw him. It grieves me, Udayin. I am an old man. Death lies in wait for me. I may live till to-morrow, but it would be rash to count on the days that follow after. And before I die, Udayin, I want to see my son. You were once his best friend; go to him now. I can think of no one who would be more welcome. Tell him of my grief; tell him of my wish, and may he not be indifferent!"

"I shall go, my lord," replied Udayin.

He went. Long before he arrived at the Bamboo Grove, he had made up his mind to become a monk, but King Suddhodana's words had affected him deeply, and he thought, "I shall tell the Master of his father's grief. He will be moved to pity and will go to him."

The Master was happy to see Udayin become one of his disciples.

Winter was almost over. It was a favorable time to travel, and Udayin said to the Buddha, one day:

"The trees are budding; they will soon be in leaf. See the bright rays of the sun shining through the branches. Master, this is a good time to travel. It is no longer cold, nor it is yet too warm; and the earth wears a lovely mantle of green. We shall have no trouble finding food on the way. Master, this is a good time to travel."

The Master smiled at Udayin and asked:

"Why do you urge me to travel, Udayin?"

"Your father, King Suddohana, would be happy to see you, Master."

The Buddha considered a moment, then he said:

"I shall go to Kapilavastu; I shall go and see my father."

11

WHEN Vimbasara heard that the Master was leaving the Bamboo Grove, to be gone for some time, he went to see him with his son, Prince Ajatasatru.

The Master looked at the young prince; then turning to the king, he said:

"May Ajatasatru be worthy of your love, O king."

Again he looked at the prince, and he said to him:

"Now listen well, Ajatasatru, and ponder my words. Cunning does not always succeed; wickedness does not always prevail. A story will prove this, the story of something that happened long ago, something I saw with my own eyes. I was then living in a forest; I was a tree-God. This tree grew between two pools, one small and unattractive, the other wide and beautiful. The little pool was full of fish; in the larger one, lotuses grew in great profusion. During a certain summer of oppressive heat, the little pool almost completely dried up; while the large pool, sheltered from the sun as it was by the lotuses, always had plenty of water and remained pleasantly cool. A crane, passing between these two pools, saw the fish and stopped. Standing on one leg, he began to think: 'These fish would be a lawful prize. But they are quick; they are likely to escape if I attack them too hastily. I must use cunning Poor fish! They are so uncomfortable in this dried-up pool! And over there is that other pool, full of deep, cool water, where they could swim about to their heart's content!' A fish saw the crane deep in thought and looking as solemn as a hermit, and he asked, 'What are you doing there, venerable bird? You seem immersed in thought.' 'I am meditating, O fish,' said the crane, 'yes, indeed, I am meditating. I am wondering how you and your friends can escape your sad fate.' 'Our sad fate! What do you mean?' 'You suffer in that shallow water, O unhappy fish! And each day, as the heat becomes more intense, the water will fall still further, and then what will become of you? For presently the pool will be completely dry, and you will all perish! Poor, poor fish! I weep for you.' All the fish had heard what the crane said. They were filled with dismay. 'What will become of us,' they cried, 'when the heat will have dried up the pool?' They turned to the crane. 'Bird, O venerable bird, can you not save us?' The crane again pretended to be lost in thought; finally, he

replied, 'I believe I see a way out of your misery.'
The fish listened eagerly. The crane said, 'There is
a marvellous pool quite near here. It is considerably
larger than the one in which you live, and the lotuses that cover the surface have protected the water from the summer's thirst. Take my word for it,
go live in that pool. I can pick you up in my bill,
one at a time, and carry you there. In that way,
you will all be saved.' The fish were happy. They
were about to accept the crane's suggestion when
a crayfish spoke up. 'I have never heard anything
quite so strange,' he exclaimed. The fish asked him,
'What is there to astonish you about that?' 'Never,'
said the crayfish, 'never, since the beginning of the
world, did I know a crane to take an interest in fish,
unless it was perhaps to eat them.' The crane assumed an offended air and said, 'What, you wicked
crayfish, you suspect me of trying to deceive these
poor fish who are in imminent danger of death!
O fish, I only want to save you; it is your welfare I seek. Put my good faith to a test if you
wish. Choose one of your number, and I shall carry
him in my bill to the lotus pool. He will see it; he
can even swim around a few times; then I shall pick
him up and bring him back here. He will tell you
what to think of me.' 'That seems quite fair,' said
the fish. To make this trip to the pool, they chose
one of the older fish who, although half blind, was

considered quite a sage. The crane carried him to
the pool, dropped him in, and let him swim about
as much as he pleased. The old fish was delighted,
and when he returned to his friends, he had only
words of praise for the crane. The fish were now
convinced that they would owe their lives to him.
'Take us,' they cried, 'take us and carry us to the
lotus pool.' 'Just as you wish,' said the crane, and
with his bill he again picked up the old, half-blind
fish. But this time he did not carry him to the pool.
Instead, he dropped him on the ground and stabbed
him with his bill; then he ate him and left the bones
at the foot of a tree, the tree of which I was the
God. This done, the crane returned to the small
pool and said, 'Who will come with me now?' The
fish were eager to see their new home, and the
crane had only to make a choice that would satisfy
his appetite. Presently, he had eaten them all, one
after another. Only the crayfish remained. The
crayfish had already shown that he distrusted the
bird, and he was now saying to himself, 'I doubt
very much that the fish are in the lotus pool. I am
afraid the crane has taken advantage of their faith
in him. Still, it would be well for me to leave this
miserable pool and go to the other one which is so
much larger and more comfortable. The crane must
carry me, but I must run no risk. And if he has deceived the others, I must avenge them.' The bird

approached the crayfish. 'It is your turn, now,' said the crane. 'How will you carry me?' asked the crayfish. 'In my bill, like the others,' replied the crane. 'No, no,' said the crayfish; 'my shell is slippery; I might fall out of your bill. Rather, let me hold on to your neck with my claws; I shall be careful not to hurt you.' The crane agreed. He stopped at the foot of the tree. 'What are you doing?' asked the crayfish. 'We are only half-way. Are you tired? Yet the distance is not great between the two pools!' The crane was at a loss for an answer. Besides, the crayfish was beginning to tighten the hold on his neck. 'And what have we here!' exclaimed the crayfish. 'This pile of fish-bones at the foot of the tree is evidence of your treachery. But you will not deceive me as you deceived the others. I shall kill you, if I must die in the attempt.' The crayfish tightened his claws. The crane was in great pain; with tears in his eyes, he cried, 'Dear crayfish, do not hurt me. I shall not eat you. I shall carry you to the pool.' 'Then go,' said the crayfish. The crane walked to the edge of the pool and extended his neck over the water. The crayfish had only to drop into the pool. Instead, he tightened his grip, and so powerful were his claws that the crane's neck was severed. And the tree-God could not help exclaiming, 'Well done, crayfish!'" The Master added: "Cunning does not always succeed. Wickedness does not always prevail. Sooner or later the treacherous crane meets a crayfish. Always remember that, Prince Ajatasatru!"

Vimbasara thanked the Master for the valuable lesson he had taught his son. Then he said:

"Blessed One, I have a request to make."

"Speak," said the Buddha.

"When you are gone, O Blessed One, I shall be unable to do you honor, I shall be unable to make you the customary offerings, and it will grieve me. Give me a lock of your hair, give me the parings of your finger-nails; I shall place them in a temple in the midst of my palace. Thus, I shall retain something that is a part of you, and, each day, I shall decorate the temple with fresh garlands, and I shall burn rare incense."

The Blessed One gave the king these things for which he had asked, and he said:

"Take my hair and take these parings; keep them in a temple, but, in your mind, keep what I have taught you."

And as Vimbasara joyfully returned to his palace, the Master left for Kapilavastu.

12

IT was a great distance from Rajagriha to Kapilavastu, and the Master was walking slowly. Udayin decided to go ahead and inform Suddhodana that his son was on his way to see him, for the king would then be patient and would cease to grieve.

Udayin flew through the air, and, in a trice, had arrived at Suddhodana's palace. He found the king in deep despair.

"My lord," said he, "dry your tears. Your son will be in Kapilavastu before long."

"Oh, it is you, Udayin!" exclaimed the king. "I thought that you, too, had forgotten to deliver my message, and I had given up hope of ever seeing my beloved son. But you have come at last, and joyful is the news you bring. I shall weep no more; I shall now patiently await the blessed moment when these eyes shall look again upon my son."

He ordered that Udayin be served a splendid repast.

"I will not eat here, my lord," said Udayin. "Before I touch any food, I must know if my master has been properly served. I shall return to him the way I came."

The king protested.

"It is my wish, Udayin, that you receive your food from me, each day; and it is also my wish that my son receive his food from me, each day of this journey which he has undertaken to please me. Eat, and I shall then give you food to take to the Blessed One."

When Udayin had eaten, he was given a bowl of delicious food to take to the king's son. He tossed the bowl into the air; then he rose from the ground and flew away. The bowl fell at the Buddha's feet, and the Buddha thanked his friend. Each day thereafter, Udayin flew to the palace of King Suddhodana to fetch the Master's food, and the Master was pleased with the zeal his disciple showed in serving him.

He finally arrived at Kapilavastu. To receive him, the Sakyas had assembled in a park bright with flowers. Many of those present were extremely proud, and they thought, "There are some here who are older than Siddhartha! Why should they pay him homage? Let the children, let the young men and young maidens, bow before him; his elders will hold their heads high!"

The Blessed One entered the park. All eyes were dazzled by the brilliant light he diffused. King

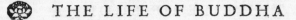

Suddhodana was deeply moved; he made a few steps in his direction. "My son . . ." he cried. His voice faltered; tears of joy coursed down his cheeks, and he slowly bowed his head.

And when the Sakyas saw the father paying homage to the son, they all humbly prostrated themselves.

A magnificent seat had been prepared for the Master. He sat down. Then the sky opened, and a shower of roses descended on the park. Earth and atmosphere were impregnated with the perfume. The king and all the Sakyas gazed in wonderment. And the Master spoke.

"I have already, in some former existence, seen my family grouped around me and heard them sing my praises as with one voice. At that time King Sanjaya was reigning in the city of Jayatura. His wife's name was Phusati, and they had a son, Visvantara. When he came of age, Visvantara married Madri, a princess of rare beauty. She bore him two children: a son, Jalin, and a daughter, Krishnajina. Visvantara owned a white elephant that had the marvellous power to make the rain fall at will. Now, the distant kingdom of Kalinga was visited by a terrible drought. The grass withered; the trees bore no fruit; men and beasts died of hunger and of thirst. The king of Kalinga heard of Visvantara's elephant and of the strange power it possessed. He sent eight brahmans to Jayatura to get it and return with it to their unfortunate country. The brahmans arrived during a festival. Riding on the elephant, the prince was on his way to the temple, to distribute alms. He saw these envoys of the foreign king. 'What brings you here?' he asked them. 'My lord,' replied the brahmans, 'our kingdom, the kingdom of Kalinga, has been visited by drought and famine. Your elephant can save us, by bringing us the rain; will you part with him?' 'It is little you ask,' said Visvantara. 'You could have asked me for my eyes or my flesh! Yes, take the elephant, and may a refreshing rain fall upon your fields and upon your gardens!' He gave the elephant to the brahmans, and they joyfully returned to Kalinga. But the inhabitants of Jayatura were greatly distressed; they feared a drought in their own country. They complained to King Sanjaya. 'My lord,' said they, 'your son's action was reprehensible. His elephant protected us from famine. What will become of us now, if the sky withholds its rain? Show him no mercy, O king; let Visvantara pay for this folly with his life.' The king wept. He tried to put them off with promises, and at first they would not listen, but they finally relented and asked that the prince be exiled to some remote and rocky desert. The king was obliged to give his consent. 'When my son hears of his exile,' thought Sanjaya, 'he will take it to heart.' But this was not the case. Visvantara simply said, 'I shall leave tomorrow, father, and I shall take none of my treasures with me.' Then he went to look for Madri, his princess. 'Madri,' said he, 'I must leave the city; my father has exiled me to a cruel desert, where it will be hard to find a livelihood. Do not come with me, O beloved; too great are the hardships you will have to endure. You will have to leave the children behind, and they will die of loneliness. Stay here with them; remain on your golden throne; it was I my father exiled, not you.' 'My lord,' replied the princess, 'if you leave me behind I shall kill myself, and the crime will lie at your door.' Visvantara was silent. He gazed at Madri; he embraced her. 'Come,' said he. Madri thanked him, and she added, 'I shall take the children with me; I can not leave them here, to die of loneliness.' The following day, Visvantara had his chariot made ready; he got in with Madri, Jalin and Krishnajina, and as they drove out of the city, King Sanjaya and Queen Phusati wept and sobbed pitifully. The prince, his wife and the children were already far from the city when they saw a brahman approaching. 'Traveller,' said the brahman, 'is this the road to Jayatura?' 'Yes,' replied Visvantara, 'but why are you going to Jayatura?' 'I come from a distant country,' said the brahman. 'I heard that there lived in Jayatura a generous prince named Visvantara. He once owned a marvellous elephant that he gave to the king of Kalinga. He is very charitable, they say. I want to see this kindly man; I want to ask him for a donation. I know that no one has ever appealed to him in vain.' Visvantara said to the brahman, 'I am the man you seek; I am Visvantara, son of King Sanjaya. Because I gave my elephant to the king of Kalinga, my father sent me into exile. What can I give you, O brahman?' When he heard these words, the brahman complained bitterly. He said in a pitiful voice: 'So they deceived me! I left my home, full of hope, and, disappointed, I must now return!' Visvantara interrupted him. 'Console yourself, brahman. Not in vain have you appealed to Prince Visvantara.' He unharnessed the horses and gave them to him. The brahman thanked his benefactor and left. Visvantara then continued on his way. He was now drawing the chariot himself. Presently, he saw another brahman approaching. He was a little, frail old man, with white hair and yellow teeth. 'Traveller,' he said to the prince, 'is this the road to Jayatura?' 'Yes,' replied the prince, 'but why are you going to Jayatura?' 'The king of that city has a son, Prince Visvantara,' said the brahman. 'Visvantara, according to the stories I have heard, is extremely charitable; he saved the kingdom of Kalinga from famine, and whatever is asked of him is never refused. I shall go to Visvantara, and I know he will not deny my request.' 'If you go to Jayatura,' said the prince, 'you will not see Visvantara; his father has exiled him to the desert.' 'Woe is me!' cried the brahman. 'Who now will help me in my feeble old age? All hope has fled, and I shall return to my home as poor as when I left!' He wept. 'Do not weep,' said Visvantara; 'I am the man you seek. You have not met me in vain. Madri, Jalin, Krishnajina, get down from the chariot! It is no longer mine: I have given it to this old man.' The brahman was overjoyed. The four exiles continued on their way. They were now on foot, and when the children were tired, Visvantara would carry Jalin, and Madri Krishnajina. A few days later, they saw a third brahman approaching. He was going to Jayatura to see Prince Visvantara and ask him for alms. The prince stripped himself of his clothes, in order that the brahman should not leave him empty-handed. Then he walked on. And a fourth brahman approached. His skin was dark, his glance fierce and imperious. 'Tell me,' he said in a harsh voice, 'is this the road to Jayatura?' 'Yes,' replied the prince, 'and what takes you to Jayatura?' The brahman wanted to see Visvantara, who was sure to give him a magnificent present. When he learned that he was in the presence of the unhappy, exiled prince, he did not weep; in an angry voice, he said, 'It was a hard road I travelled, and it must not have been in vain. You have undoubtedly brought along some valuable jewelry which you can give me.' Madri was wearing a necklace of gold. Visvantara asked her for it; she smiled and handed it to him, and the brahman took the necklace and went away. Visvantara, Madri, Jalin and Krishnajina kept on walking. They crossed raging torrents; they ascended ravines covered with underbrush; they travelled over rocky plains seared by a merciless sun. Madri's feet were cut by the stones; Visvantara's heels were worn to the bone, and wherever they passed, they left a trail of blood. One day, Visvantara, who was walking ahead, heard some one sobbing. He turned around and saw Madri sitting on the ground, lamenting her fate. He was seized with anguish, and he said, 'I begged and pleaded with you, my beloved, not to follow me into exile, but you would not listen. Come, stand up; however great our weariness, the children must not suffer for it; we must not mind our wounds.' Madri saw that his feet were bleeding, and she cried, 'Oh, how much greater is your suffering than mine! I shall control my grief.' She tried to stand up, but her limbs gave way, and once again she burst into tears. 'All my strength has left me,' she sobbed; 'even the love I bear my husband and my children is not enough to sustain my courage. I shall die of hunger and of thirst in this dreadful land; my children will die, and perhaps my well-beloved.' From the sky, Indra had been watching Visvantara and his family. He was touched by Madri's grief, and he decided to come down to earth. He assumed the form of a pleasant old man, and, astride a swift horse, he advanced to meet the prince. He accosted Visvantara and addressed him in an engaging manner. 'From your appearance it is evident, my lord, that you have suffered great hardship. There is a city not far from here. I shall show you the way. You and your family must come to my home and stay as long as you please.' The old man was smiling. He urged the four exiles to get on his horse, and as Visvantara seemed to hesitate, he said, 'The horse is powerful, and you are not heavy. As for me, I shall walk; it will not tire me, for we have not far to go.' Visvantara was astonished to learn that a city had been built in this cruel desert; besides, he had never heard of the city. But the old man's voice was so pleasant that he decided to follow him, and Madri was so weary that he accepted the invitation to ride with her and the children. They had gone about three hundred paces when a magnificent city ap-

peared before them. It was immense. A wide river
flowed through it, and there were many beautiful
gardens and orchards full of ripe fruit. The old
man led his guests to the gates of a shining palace.
'Here is my home,' said he; 'here, if you wish, you
may dwell the rest of your days. Please enter.' In
the great hall, Visvantara and Madri sat on thrones
of gold; at their feet, the children played on heavy
rugs, and the old man presented them with many
beautiful robes. Exquisite food was then served to
them, and they appeased their hunger. But Visvantara was lost in thought. Suddenly, he rose from
his seat, and he said to the old man, 'My lord, I am
disobeying my father's commands. He banished me
from Jayatura, where he is king, and he ordered me
to spend the rest of my life in the desert. I must
not enjoy these comforts, for they were forbidden.
My lord, permit me to leave your house.' The old
man tried to dissuade him, but it was futile; and
followed by Madri and the children, Visvantara
left the city. Outside the gates, he turned around
to take a last look, but the city had disappeared;
where it had once stood, there was now only burning sand. And Visvantara was happy that he had
not remained longer. He finally came to a mountain, overrun by an immense forest, and there he
found a hut that a hermit had once occupied. Out
of leaves, he made a couch for himself and his fam-

ily, and there, at last, undisturbed by remorse, he
found rest and peace. Every day, Madri went into
the forest to gather wild fruit; it was the only food
they had, and they drank the water of a clear, bub-
bling spring they had discovered near the hut. For
seven months they saw no one; then, one day, a
brahman passed by. Madri was away, gathering
fruit, and Visvantara was watching the children
while they played in front of the hut. The brahman stopped and observed them carefully. 'Friend,'
he said to the father, 'will you give me your children?' Visvantara was so taken aback that he was
unable to reply. He glanced anxiously at the brahman and finally questioned him. 'Yes, will you give
me your children? I have a wife, much younger
than myself. She is rather a haughty woman. She is
tired of doing household work, and she asked me to
find two children who could be her slaves. Why not
give me yours? You seem to be very poor; it must
be hard for you to feed them. In my home they
will have plenty to eat, and I shall try to have my
wife treat them as kindly as possible.' Visvantara
thought, 'What a painful sacrifice I am being asked
to make. What shall I do? In spite of what the brahman says, my children will be very unhappy in his
home; his wife is cruel, she will beat them and will
give them only scraps of food. But since he has
asked me for them, have I the right to refuse?' He

thought a while longer, then he finally said, 'Take the children with you, brahman; let them be your wife's slaves.' And Jalin and Krishnajina, their faces wet with tears, went away with the brahman. Madri, in the meanwhile, had been gathering pomegranates, but each time she picked one off the tree, it slipped out of her hand. This frightened her, and she hurried back to the hut. She missed the children, and turning to her husband she asked, 'Where are the children?' Visvantara was sobbing. 'Where are the children?' Still no reply. She repeated the question a third time. 'Where are the children?' And she added, 'Answer, answer quickly. Your silence is killing me.' Visvantara spoke; in a pitiful voice, he said, 'A brahman came; he wanted the children for slaves!' 'And you gave them to him!' cried Madri. 'Could I refuse?' Madri swooned; she was unconscious a long time. When she recovered, her lamentations were pitiful. She cried, 'Oh, my children, you who would rouse me from my slumber at night; you who would be given the choicest fruit I had gathered, a wicked man has taken you away! I can see him forcing you to run, you who have just learned to walk. In his home, you will go hungry; you will be brutally beaten. You will be working in the house of a stranger. You will furtively watch the roads, but neither father nor mother will you ever

see again. And your lips will be parched; your feet
will be hurt by the sharp stones; the sun will burn
your cheeks. Oh, my children, we were always able
to spare you the hardships we had to endure. We
carried you across the fearful desert; you did not
suffer then, but now, what will you suffer?' She
was still weeping when another brahman came
through the forest. He was an old man and walked
with great difficulty. He stared at the princess with
watery eyes, then he addressed Prince Visvantara.
'My lord, as you see, I am old and feeble. I have no
one at home to help me when I get up in the morning or when I go to bed at night; I have neither
son nor daughter to look after me. Now, this
woman is young; she seems quite strong. Let me
take her for a servant. She will help me to get up;
she will put me to bed; she will watch over me
while I sleep. Give me this woman, my lord; you
will be doing a good deed, a saintly deed, that will
be praised throughout the world.' Visvantara had
listened attentively; he was pensive. He looked at
Madri. 'Beloved, you heard what the brahman
said; what would you answer?' She replied, 'Since
you have given away our children: Jalin, the best-
beloved, and darling Krishnajina, you can give me
to this brahman; I shall not complain.' Visvantara
took Madri's hand and placed it in the brahman's
hand. He felt no remorse; he was not even weeping.

The brahman received the woman; he thanked the prince and said, 'May you know great glory, Visvantara; may you become the Buddha some dav!' He started away, but turned, suddenly, and came back to the hut. And he said, 'I shall look for a servant in some other land; I shall leave this woman here, to remain with the Gods of the mountain, and the Goddesses of the forest and of the spring; and, hereafter, you must give her to no one.' While the old brahman was speaking, his appearance gradually changed; he became very beautiful; his face was gloriously radiant. Visvantara and Madri recognized Indra. They fell at his feet and worshipped him; and the God said to them, 'Each one of you may ask one favor of me, and it shall be granted.' Visvantara said, 'Oh, that I might become the Buddha some day and bring deliverance to those who are born and who die in the mountains!' Indra replied, 'Glory be to you who, one day, shall be the Buddha!' Madri spoke next. 'My lord, grant me this favor: may the brahman, to whom my children were given, decide to sell them instead of keeping them in his home, may he find a buyer only in Jayatura, and may that buyer be Sanjaya himself.' Indra replied, 'So be it!' As he ascended to the sky, Madri murmured, 'Oh, that King Sanjaya might forgive his son!' And she heard the God say, 'So be it!' In the meantime, Jalin and Krishnajina had arrived at their new home. The brahman's wife was very pleased with these two young slaves, and she lost no time putting them to work. She delighted in giving orders, and the children had to obey her slightest whim. At first, they did their best to carry out her wishes, but she was such an exacting mistress that they soon lost all desire to please, and many were the reprimands and the blows they received. The more harshly they were treated, the more discouraged they became, and the woman finally said to the brahman, 'I can do nothing with these children. Sell them and bring me other slaves, slaves who know how to work and obey.' The brahman took the children and went from city to city, trying to sell them, but no one would buy: the price was too high. He finally arrived in Jayatura. One of the king's counsellors passed them in the street; he stared at the children, at their emaciated bodies and sun-burned faces, and, suddenly, he recognized them by their eyes. He stopped the brahman and asked, 'Where did you get these children?' 'I got them in a mountain forest, my lord,' replied the brahman. 'They were given to me for slaves; they were unruly, and I am now trying to sell them.' The king's counsellor became anxious; turning to the children, he asked, 'Does this servitude mean that your father is dead?' 'No,' replied Jalin, 'both our parents are alive, but father gave us to this brahman.' The counsellor ran to the palace of the king. 'My lord,' he cried, 'Visvantara has given your grandchildren, Jalin and Krishnajina, to a brahman. They are his slaves. He is dissatisfied with their service, and is taking them from city to city, in order to sell them!' King Sanjaya ordered the brahman and the children brought before him at once. They were soon found, and when the king saw the misery that had come to these children of his race, he wept bitter tears. Jalin addressed him in a pleading voice. 'Buy us, my lord, for we are unhappy in the brahman's home, and we want to live with you, who love us. But do not take us by force; our father gave us to the brahman, and from this sacrifice he expects to receive great blessings, for himself and for all creatures.' 'What price do you want for these children?' the king asked the brahman. 'You may have them for a thousand head of cattle,' replied the brahman. 'Very well.' The king turned to his counsellor and said, 'You who will now rank next to me in my kingdom, give this brahman a thousand head of cattle, and pay him also a thousand measures of gold.' Then the king, accompanied by Jalin and Krishnajina, went to Queen Phu-

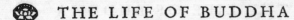

sati. At the sight of her grandchildren, she laughed
and wept for joy; she dressed them in costly clothes,
and she gave them rings and necklaces to wear.
Then she asked them about their father and mother.
'They live in a rude hut, in a forest, on the slope of
a mountain,' said Jalin. 'They have given away all
their possessions. They live on fruit and water, and
their only companions are the wild beasts of the
forest.' 'Oh, my lord' cried Phusati, 'will you not
recall your son from exile?' King Sanjaya sent a
messenger to Prince Visvantara; he pardoned him,
and ordered him to return to Jayatura. When the
prince drew near the city, he saw his father, his
mother and his children advancing to greet him.
They were accompanied by a great crowd of people
who had heard of Visvantara's sufferings and of his
virtue, and who now forgave him and admired
him. And the king said to the prince, 'Dear son, I
have done you a grave injustice; know my remorse.
Be kind to me: forget my blunder; and be kind to
the inhabitants of the city: forget that they ever
wronged you. Never again will your acts of charity
give us offense.' Visvantara smiled and embraced his
father, while Madri fondled Jalin and Krishnajina,
and Phusati wept for joy. And when the prince
passed through the gates of the city, he was acclaimed as with one voice. Now, Visvantara was I,
O Sakyas! You acclaimed me as they once ac-

claimed him. Walk in the path that leads to deliverance."

The Blessed One was silent. The Sakyas had listened attentively; they now bowed before him and withdrew. However, not one of them had thought of offering him his meal on the morrow.

She ascended to the terrace of the palace. Surrounded by a crowd of people, the Master was approaching. A majestic splendor emanated from his

13

T HE following day, the Master went through
the city, begging his food from house to
house. He was soon recognized, and the
people of Kapilavastu exclaimed:

"What a strange sight! Prince Siddhartha, who
once drove through these streets, dressed in magnificent robes, now wanders from door to door,
begging his food, in the humble garb of a monk."

And they rushed to the windows; they ascended
to the terraces, and great was their admiration for
the beggar.

One of Gopa's maidens heard the excitement as
she was leaving the palace. She asked the reason and
was told. She immediately ran back to her mistress.

"Your husband, Prince Siddhartha," said she,
"is wandering through the city, like a mendicant
monk!"

Gopa gave a start. She thought, "He who once,
for all his gorgeous jewels, was radiant with light,
now wears coarse clothes, now has for sole adorn-
ment the divine brilliance of his person." And she
murmured, "How beautiful he must be!"

175

She ascended to the terrace of the palace. Surrounded by a crowd of people, the Master was approaching. A majestic splendor emanated from his person. Gopa trembled with joy, and in a voice full of fervor she sang:

"Soft and shining is his hair, brilliant as the sun his forehead, radiant and smiling his sweeping glance! He stalks like a lion through the golden light!"

She went to the king.

"My lord," said she, "your son is begging in the streets of Kapilavastu. An admiring throng follows him about, for he is more beautiful than ever before."

Suddhodana was greatly disturbed. He left the palace, and approaching his son, he said to him:

"What are you doing? Why do you beg your food? Surely you must know that I expect you at the palace, you and your disciples."

"I must beg," replied the Blessed One; "I must obey the law."

"We are a race of warriors," said the king; "no Sakya was ever a beggar."

"You belong to the Sakya race; I, in the course of my previous existences, have sought supreme knowledge; I have learned the beauty of charity; I have known the joy of self-sacrifice. When I was the child Dharmapala, the queen, my mother, was

176

playing with me one day, and she forgot to greet my father, King Brahmadatta, as he passed by. In order to punish her, he ordered one of the guards to cut off my hands, for he thought it would hurt her more to see me suffer than to suffer herself. My mother pleaded with him and offered her hands instead, but he was inexorable, and he was obeyed. I was smiling, and to see me smile, soon brought a smile to my mother's face. My father then ordered the guard to cut off my feet. This was done, and still I kept smiling. In a violent rage, he cried, 'Cut off his head!' My mother became terrified; she cowered before him. 'Cut off my head,' she begged, 'but spare your son, O king!' The king was about to yield when I spoke up in a childish voice. 'Mother, it is for your salvation that I give my head. When I am dead, let my body be placed on a pike and exposed to view; let it be food for the birds of the air.' And, as the executioner seized me by the hair, I added, 'Oh, that I might become the Buddha and set free all who are born and who die in the worlds!' And now, King Suddhodana, now at last I have attained wisdom; I am the Buddha; I know the path that leads to deliverance. Do not disturb me at my task. Be wide awake; be quick of apprehension; follow the sacred path of virtue. He sleeps in peace who leads a life of holiness, he sleeps on earth and in the other worlds."

King Suddhodana wept with admiration. The Buddha continued:

"Learn to distinguish true virtue from false virtue; learn to know the true path from the false path. He sleeps in peace who lead a life of holiness, he sleeps on earth and in the other worlds!"

The king fell at his feet; he believed in him, completely. The Blessed One smiled, then entered the palace and sat down at his father's table.

14

PRESENTLY the women of the palace came to pay homage to the Master. Gopa, alone, was missing. The king evinced his surprise.

"I asked her to come with us," said Mahaprajapati. " 'I shall not go with you,' she answered. 'I may be wanting in virtue; I may not deserve to see my husband. If I have done nothing wrong, he will come to me of his own accord, and I shall then show him the respect that is his due.' "

The Master left his seat and went to Gopa's apartments. She had discarded her costly raiment and her soft veils; she had flung aside her bracelets and her necklaces; she was wearing a reddish-colored robe, made of some coarse material. At the sight of her thus attired, he smiled with happiness. She fell at his feet and worshipped him.

"You see," said she, "I wanted to dress as you are dressed; I wanted to know about your life in order to live as you live. You eat but once a day, and I eat but once a day. You gave up sleeping in a bed; look around: no bed will you see, for here is the bench on which I sleep. And from now on

179

I shall have done with sweet perfumes, and no longer shall I put flowers in my hair."

"I was aware of your great virtue, Gopa," replied the Master. "It has not failed you, and I praise you for it. How many women are there in this world who would have had the courage to do as you did?"

And seating himself, he spoke these words:

"Women are not to be trusted. For one who is wise and good, more than a thousand can be found who are foolish and wicked. Woman is more mysterious than the path of a fish through the water; she is as fierce as a robber, and like the robber, she is deceitful; she will rarely tell the truth, for to her a lie is like the truth and the truth like a lie. Often have I told my disciples to avoid women. It displeases me even to have them speak to them. Yet you, Gopa, are not false; I believe in your virtue. Virtue is a flower not easily found; a woman must have clear eyes in order to see it; she must have pure hands in order to gather it. Mara hides his pointed arrows under flowers; oh, how many women love treacherous flowers, flowers that inflict wounds which never heal! Unhappy women! The body is but foam and they know it not. They cling to this world, then the day comes when King Death claims them for his own. The body is less substantial than a mirage: who knows that will break Mara's flowered arrows, who knows that will never meet King Death. Death carries away the woman who heedlessly gathers flowers, even as the torrent, swollen by the storm, carries away the drowsy village. Gather flowers, O woman, take joy in their colors, drink in their perfume; Death lies in wait for you, and before you are satisfied, you will be his. Consider the bee: it goes from flower to flower, and, harming no one, simply takes the nectar from which honey is made."

WHEN Siddhartha had retired from the world, King Suddhodana had chosen Nanda, another one of his sons, to succeed him to the throne. Nanda, was happy to think that one day he would be king, and he was also happy at the thought of his coming marriage to Princess Sundarika, to beautiful Sundarika whom he loved dearly.

The Master feared for his brother; he was afraid he would stray into the path of evil. One day, he he went to him and said:

"I have come to you, Nanda, because I know you are very happy, and I want to hear from your own lips the reason for this happiness. So speak, Nanda; bare your heart to me."

"Brother," replied Nanda, "I doubt if you would understand, for you once spurned sovereign power and you deserted loving Gopa!"

"You expect to be king some day, and that is why you are happy, Nanda!"

"Yes. And I am also happy because I love Sundarika, and because Sundarika will soon be my bride."

"Poor man!" cried the Master. "How can you

be happy, you who live in darkness? Would you see the light? Then first rid yourself of happiness: fear is born of happiness, fear and suffering. He neither fears nor suffers who no longer knows happiness. Rid yourself of love: fear is born of love, fear and suffering. He neither fears nor suffers who no longer knows love. If you seek happiness in the world, your efforts will come to nothing, your pleasure will turn to pain; death is always present, ready to swoop down on the unfortunate and still their laughter and their song. The world is but flame and smoke, and everything in the world suffers from birth, from old age and from death. Since you first began pitifully to wander from existence to existence, you have shed more tears than there is water in the rivers or in the seas. You have grieved and you have wept at being thwarted in your desires, and you have wept and you have grieved when that happened which you dreaded. A mother's death, a father's death, a brother's death, a sister's death, the death of a son, the death of a daughter, oh, how many times, down through the ages, have these not caused you heartache? And how many times have you not lost your fortune? And each time you had cause for grief, you wept and you wept and you wept, and you have shed more tears than there is water in the rivers or in the seas!"

Nanda, at first, paid little heed to what the Buddha was saying, but as he began to listen the words moved him deeply. The Master continued:

"Look upon the world as a bubble of foam; let it be but a dream, and sovereign death will pass you by."

He was silent.

"Master, Master," cried Nanda, "I will be your disciple! Take me with you."

The Master took Nanda by the hand and left the palace. But Nanda was pensive; he was afraid he had been hasty. Perhaps he would bitterly regret what he had done. For whatever might be said of it, it was pleasant and noble to exercise sovereign power. And Sundarika? "How beautiful she is," he thought; "shall I ever see her again?" And he uttered a deep sigh.

But he still followed the Master. He was afraid to speak to him. He feared his rebuke as he feared his scorn.

Suddenly, as they turned the corner of a street, he saw a young girl approaching. She was smiling. He recognized Sundarika, and he lowered his eyes.

"Where are you going?" she asked him.

He did not answer. She turned to the Master.

"Are you taking him with you?"

"Yes," replied the Master.

"But he will come back soon?"

Nanda wanted to cry, "Yes, I shall come back soon, Sundarika!" But he was afraid, and without a word, his eyes still downcast, he went off with the Master.

Then Sundarika knew that Nanda was lost to her, and she wept.

16

ONE day, gentle Gopa stood looking at her son Rahula.

"How beautiful you are, my child!" she exclaimed. "How your eyes sparkle! Your father owes you a pious heritage; you must go and claim it."

Mother and child ascended to the terrace of the palace. The Blessed One was passing in the street below. Gopa said to Rahula:

"Rahula, do you see that monk?"

"Yes, mother," replied the child. "His body is covered with gold."

"He is as beautiful as the Gods of the sky! It is the light of holiness that makes his skin shine like gold. Love him, my son, love him dearly, for he is your father. He once possessed great treasures; he had gold and silver and glittering jewels; now, he goes from house to house, begging his food. But he has acquired a marvellous treasure: he has attained supreme knowledge. Go to him, my son; tell him who you are, and demand your heritage."

Rahula obeyed his mother. He was presently

standing before the Buddha. He felt strangely happy.

"Monk," said he, "it is nice to stand here, in your shadow."

The Master looked at him. It was a kindly glance, and Rahula, taking heart, began walking beside him. Remembering his mother's words, he said:

"I am your son, my Lord. I know that you possess the greatest of treasures. Father, give me my heritage."

The Master smiled. He made no reply. He continued to beg. But Rahula remained at his side; he followed him about and kept repeating:

"Father, give me my heritage."

At last the Master spoke:

"Child, you know nothing about this treasure that you have heard men praise. When you claim your heritage, you think you are claiming material things of a perishable nature. The only treasures known to you are those dear to human vanity, treasures that greedy death wrests from the false rich. But why should you be kept in ignorance? You are right to claim your heritage, Rahula. You shall have your share of the jewels that are mine. You shall see the seven jewels; you shall know the seven virtues, and you shall learn the true value of faith and purity, modesty and reserve, obedience, abnegation and wisdom. Come, I shall give you in charge of holy Sariputra; he will teach you."

Rahula went with his father, and Gopa rejoiced. King Suddhodana, alone, was sad: his family was deserting him! He could not help speaking his mind to the Master.

"Do not grieve," replied the Master, "for great is the treasure they will share who hearken to my words and follow me! Bear your grief in silence; be like the elephant wounded in battle by the arrows of the enemy: no one hears him complain. Kings ride into battle on elephants that are under perfect control; in the world, the great man is the man who has learned to control himself, the man who bears his grief in silence. He who is truly humble, he who curbs his passions as one curbs wild horses, is envied by the Gods. He does no evil. Neither in the mountain-caves nor in the caverns of the sea can you escape the consequences of an evil deed; they follow you about; they sear you; they drive you mad, for they give you no peace! But if you do good, when you leave the earth your good deeds greet you, like friends upon your return from a voyage. We live in perfect happiness, we who are without hatred in a world full of hatred. We live in perfect happiness, we who are without sickness in a world full of sickness. We live in perfect happiness, we who are without weariness in a world full of weariness. We live in perfect happiness, we who possess nothing. Joy is our food, and we are like radiant Gods. The monk who lives in solitude preserves a soul that is full of peace; he contemplates the truth with a clear, steady gaze, and enjoys a felicity unknown to ordinary mortals."

Having consoled King Suddhodana with these words, the Blessed One left Kapilavastu and returned to Rajagriha.

17

THE Master was in Rajagriha when a rich merchant named Anathapindika arrived from Cravasti. Anathapindika was a religious man, and when he heard that a Buddha was living in the Bamboo Grove, he was eager to see him.

He set out one morning, and as he entered the Grove, a divine voice led him to where the Master was seated. He was greeted with words of kindness; he presented the community with a magnificent gift, and the Master promised to visit him in Cravasti.

When he returned home, Anathapindika began to wonder where he could receive the Blessed One. His gardens did not seem worthy of such a guest. The most beautiful park in the city belonged to Prince Jeta, and Anathapindika decided to buy it.

"I will sell the park," Jeta said to him, "if you cover the ground with gold coins."

Anathapindika accepted the terms. He had chariot-loads of gold coins carried to the park, and presently only a small strip of ground remained uncovered. Then Jeta joyfully exclaimed:

"The park is yours, merchant; I will gladly give you the strip that is still uncovered."

Anathapindika had the park made ready for the Master; then he sent his most faithful servant to the Bamboo Grove, to inform him that he was now prepared to receive him in Cravasti.

"O Venerable One," said the messenger, "my master falls at your feet. He hopes you have been spared anxiety and sickness, and that you are not loath to keep the promise you made to him. You are awaited in Cravasti, O Venerable One."

The Blessed One had not forgotten the promise he had made to the merchant Anathapindika; he wished to abide by it, and he said to the messenger, "I will go."

He allowed a few days to pass; then he took his cloak and his alms-bowl, and followed by a great number of disciples, he set out for Cravasti. The messenger went ahead, to tell the merchant he was coming.

Anathapindika decided to go and meet the Master. His wife, his son and his daughter accompanied him, and they were attended by the wealthiest inhabitants of the city. And when they saw the Buddha, they were dazzled by his splendor; he seemed to be walking on a path of molten gold.

They escorted him to Jeta's park, and Anatha-pindika said to him:

"My Lord, what shall I do with this park?"

"Give it to the community, now and for all time," replied the Master.

Anathapindika ordered a servant to bring him a golden bowl full of water. He poured the water over the Master's hands, and he said:

"I give this park to the community, ruled by the Buddha, now and for all time."

"Good!" said the Master. "I accept the gift. This park will be a happy refuge; here we shall live in peace, and find shelter from the heat and from the cold. No vicious animals enter here: not even the humming of a mosquito disturbs the silence; and here there is protection from the rain, the biting wind and the ardent sun. And this park will inspire dreams, for here we shall meditate hour after hour. It is only right that such gifts be made to the community. The intelligent man, the man who does not neglect his own interests, should give the monks a proper home; he should give them food and drink; he should give them clothes. The monks, in return, will teach him the law, and he who knows the law is delivered from evil and attains nirvana."

The Buddha and his disciples established themselves in Jeta's park,

Anathapindika was happy; but, one day, a solemn thought occurred to him.

"I am being loudly praised," he said to himself, "and yet what is so admirable about my actions? I present gifts to the Buddha and to the monks, and for this I am entitled to a future reward; but my virtue benefits me alone! I must get others to share in the privilege. I shall go through the streets of the city, and from those whom I meet, I shall get donations for the Buddha and for the monks. Many will thus participate in the good I shall be doing."

He went to Prasenajit, king of Cravasti, who was a wise and upright man. He told him what he had decided to do, and the king approved. A herald was sent through the city with this royal proclamation:

"Listen well, inhabitants of Cravasti! Seven days from this day, the merchant Anathapindika, riding an elephant, will go through the streets of the city. He will ask all of you for alms, which he will then offer to the Buddha and to his disciples. Let each one of you give him whatever he can afford."

On the day announced, Anathapindika mounted his finest elephant and rode through the streets, asking every one for donations for the Master and for the community. They crowded around him: this one gave gold, that one silver; one woman took off her necklace, another her bracelet, a third an anklet; and even the humblest gifts were accepted.

Now, there lived in Cravasti a young girl who was extremely poor. It had taken her three months to save enough money to buy a piece of coarse material, out of which she had just made a dress for herself. She saw Anathapindika with a great crowd around him.

"The merchant Anathapindika appears to be begging," she said to a bystander.

"Yes, he is begging," was the reply.

"But he is said to be the richest man in Cravasti. Why should he be begging?"

"Did you not hear the royal proclamation being cried through the streets, seven days ago?"

"No."

"Anathapindika is not collecting alms for himself. He wants every one to participate in the good he is doing, and he is asking for donations for the Buddha and his disciples. All those who give will be entitled to a future reward."

The young girl said to herself, "I have never done anything deserving of praise. It would be wonderful to make an offering to the Buddha. But I am poor. What have I to give?" She walked away, wistfully. She looked at her new dress. "I have only

194

this dress to offer him. But I can not go through the streets naked."

She went home and took off the dress. Then she sat at the window and watched for Anathapindika, and when he passed in front of her house, she threw the dress to him. He took it and showed it to his servants.

"The woman who threw this dress to me," said he, "probably had nothing else to offer. She must be naked, if she had to remain at home and give alms in this strange manner. Go; try to find her and see who she is."

The servants had some difficulty finding the young girl. At last they saw her, and they learned that their master had been correct in his surmise: the dress thrown out of the window was the poor child's entire fortune. Anathapindika was deeply moved; he ordered his servants to bring many costly, beautiful clothes, and he gave them to this pious maiden who had offered him her simple dress.

She died the following day and was reborn a Goddess in Indra's sky. But she never forgot how she had come to deserve such a reward, and, one night, she came down to earth and went to the Buddha, and he instructed her in the holy law.

18

THE Master remained in Cravasti for some time; then he left, to return to Rajagriha where King Vimbasara awaited him.

He had stopped to rest in a village that was about halfway, when he saw seven men approaching. He recognized them. Six were relatives, and they were among the wealthiest and most powerful of the Sakyas. Their names were Anuruddha, Bhadrika, Bhrigu, Kimbala, Devadatta and Ananda. The seventh was a barber named Upali.

Anuruddha, one day had said to himself that it was a disgrace that none of the Sakyas had seen fit to follow the Buddha. He decided to set a good example, and as there was no reason for hiding his intention, he mentioned it first to Bhadrika, who was his best friend. Bhadrika approved of his decision, and after giving it some thought, resolved to do likewise. These two then won over Ananda, Bhrigu, Kimbala and Devadatta, by convincing them that there was no higher calling than that of a monk.

The six princes then set out to join the Buddha.

They had hardly left Kapilavastu when Ananda, glancing at Bhadrika, exclaimed:

"How now, Bhadrika! You would lead a life of holiness, and you keep all your jewels?"

Bhadrika blushed; but then he saw that Ananda was also wearing his jewelry, and he laughingly replied:

"Look at yourself, Ananda."

It was now Ananda's turn to blush.

Whereupon they all looked at one another, and they found they were still wearing their jewels. It made them feel ashamed; they lowered their eyes, and were walking along the road in silence when they met the barber Upali.

"Barber," said Ananda, "take my jewels; I give them to you."

"And take mine," said Bhadrika.

The others also handed their jewels to Upali. He was at a loss for an answer. Why should these princes, who had never seen him before, give him such presents? Should he accept them? Should he refuse?

Anuruddha understood the barber's hesitation. He said to him:

"Do not be afraid to accept these jewels. We are on our way to join the great hermit who was born to the Sakyas, we are on our way to join Siddhartha, who has become the Buddha. He will instruct us in the knowledge, and we shall submit to his rule."

"Princes," asked the barber, "are you going to become monks?"

"Yes," they answered.

He then took the jewels and started for the city. But, suddenly, he thought, "I am acting like a fool. Who will ever believe that princes thrust these riches upon me? I shall be taken for a thief, or perhaps for an assassin. The least that can happen to me is that I shall incur the deep displeasure of the Sakyas. I shall not keep the jewels." He hung them on a tree that stood beside the road. And he thought, "Those princes are setting a noble example. They had the courage to leave their palaces; do I, who am nothing, lack the courage to leave my shop? No. I shall follow them. I, too, shall see the Buddha, and may he receive me into the community!"

He followed the princes at a distance. He was shy about joining them. Bhadrika happened to turn around. He saw Upali; he called him.

"Barber, why did you throw away our jewels?" he asked.

"I, too, want to become a monk," replied the barber.

"Then walk with us," said Bhadrika.

But Upali still hung back. Anuruddha said to him:

"Walk beside us, barber. Monks make no distinctions, except for age and for virtue. When we stand before the Buddha, you must even be the first to address him, and the first to ask him to receive you into the community. For by yielding to you, the princes will show that they have put aside their Sakya pride."

They continued on their way. Suddenly, a hawk swooped down on Devadatta's head and carried off a diamond he had been wearing in his hair. This exposed his vanity, and it made the princes smile. Devadatta, now, had not a single jewel left, but his companions, in their hearts, still questioned the sincerity of his faith.

19

THE Master was happy to number these relatives among his disciples, and he took them with him to the Bamboo Grove.

There, poor Nanda was suffering. He kept thinking of Sundarika; she often appeared to him in his dreams, and he regretted having left her. The Buddha knew of his unhappiness, and he decided to cure him.

One day, he took him by the hand and led him to a tree where a hideous monkey was sitting.

"Look at that monkey," said he, "is she not beautiful?"

"I have rarely seen one as ugly," replied Nanda.

"Really?" said the Master. "And yet she resembles Sundarika, your former betrothed."

"What are you talking about!" exclaimed Nanda. "Do you mean to say that this monkey looks like Sundarika, who is grace, who is beauty itself?"

"In what way is Sundarika different? Are they not both females, do they not both awaken the desire of the male? I believe you would be willing to leave the path of holiness and run to Sundarika's

arms, just as somewhere in this wood there is a monkey that can be roused to a frenzy of love by the violent ardor of this female. They will both become old and decrepit, and then you, as well as the monkey, will wonder what could have caused your folly. They will both die, and perhaps you and the monkey will then understand the vanity of passion. Sundarika is no different from this monkey."

But Nanda was not listening. He was sighing. He was dreaming that he saw slender, graceful Sundarika wandering in a garden bright with flowers.

"Take the hem of my cloak!" the Blessed One said, imperiously.

Nanda obeyed. He felt the earth suddenly give way under him, and a fierce wind sweep him to the sky. When he regained his feet, he found himself in a marvellous park. He was walking on a path of gold, and the flowers were living jewels, fashioned out of rubies and fragrant sapphires.

"You are in Indra's sky," said the Blessed One. "Open your sightless eyes."

Nanda saw a house of shining silver surrounded by an emerald field. An Apsaras, far lovelier than Sundarika, was standing at the door. She was smiling. Maddened by desire, Nanda rushed to her, but she stopped him with a sudden gesture.

"Be pure on earth," she said to him; "keep your vows, Nanda. After your death, you will be reborn here; then you may come to my arms."

The Apsaras disappeared. Nanda and the Master returned to earth.

Nanda forgot Sundarika. He was haunted by the lovely vision he had seen in the celestial gardens, and, out of love for the Apsaras, he now resolved to lead a pure life.

But the monks still looked at him with disapproval. They would not speak to him; often, when they met him in the Bamboo Grove, they would smile at him scornfully. This made him unhappy. He thought, "They seem to bear me ill will; I wonder why?" One day, he stopped Ananda who was passing, and he asked him:

"Why do the monks avoid me? Why do you not speak to me any more, Ananda? Formerly, in Kapilavastu, we were friends as well as relatives. What have I done to offend you?"

"Poor man!" replied Ananda. "We, who meditate on the saintly truths, have been forbidden by the Master to speak to you, who meditate on the charms of an Apsaras!"

And he left.

Nanda was very disturbed. He ran to the Master; he fell at his feet and wept. The Master said to him:

"Your thoughts are evil, Nanda. You are a slave to your feelings. First it was Sundarika, now it is an Apsaras, who turns your head. And you would be reborn! Reborn among the Gods? What folly, what vanity! Strive to attain wisdom, Nanda; give heed to my teachings, and kill your devouring passions."

Nanda pondered the Buddha's words. He became a most obedient disciple, and gradually he purified his mind. Sundarika no longer appeared to him in his dreams, and now, when he thought of the Apsaras, he laughed at having wanted to become a God for her sake. One day, when he saw a hideous monkey watching him from a tree-top, he cried in a triumphant voice:

"Hail, you that Sundarika can not equal in grace; hail, you that are lovelier far than the loveliest Apsaras!"

He took great pride in having conquered his passions. "I am a true saint," he said to himself, "and in virtue I will not yield even to my brother."

He made a robe for himself of the same size as the Master's. Some monks saw him in the distance, and they said:

"Here comes the Master. Let us rise and greet him."

But as Nanda drew near, they saw their mistake.

They were embarrassed, and as they sat down again, they said:

"He has not been in the community as long as we have; why should we rise in his presence?"

Nanda had been pleased to see the monks rise at his approach; he was abashed to see them sit down again. But he was afraid to complain; he felt they would blame him. Yet it was no lesson to him; he continued to walk through the Bamboo Grove, wearing a robe that was like the Buddha's. In the distance, he was taken for the Master, and the monks would rise from their seats; but at his approach, they would laugh and sit down again.

Finally, a monk went to the Buddha and told him. He was very displeased. He assembled the monks, and in front of them all, he asked Nanda:

"Nanda, did you really wear a robe of the same size as mine?"

"Yes, Blessed One," replied Nanda; "I wore a robe of the same size as yours."

"What!" said the Master, "a disciple dares to make a robe for himself of the same size as the Buddha's! What do you mean by such audacity? An action of this kind does not tend to arouse the faith of the unbeliever, nor does it help to strengthen the faith of the believer. You must shorten your robe, Nanda, and, in the future, any monk who makes a robe for himself of the same size as the Buddha's, or larger than the Buddha's, will be committing a grave offense, an offense for which he will be severely punished."

Nanda saw the error of his ways, and he realized that to be a true saint, he would have to conquer his pride.

ℛ

NEAR the city of Vaisali, there was an immense wood that had been presented to the Master, and there he was living when the news came to him that his father, King Suddhodana, had fallen sick. The king was an old man; the illness was serious; it was feared that he was dying. The Master decided to visit him, and flying through the air he came to Kapilavastu.

The king lay mournfully on his couch. He was gasping for breath. Death was very near. Yet he smiled when he saw his son. And the Master spoke these words:

"Long is the road you have travelled, O king, and always did you strive to do good. You knew nothing of evil desires; your heart was innocent of hatred, and anger never blinded your mind. Happy is he who is given to doing good! Happy is he who looks into a limpid pool and sees his unsullied countenance, but far happier is he who examines his mind and knows the purity thereof! Your mind is pure, O king, and your death as calm as the close of a lovely day."

"Blessed One," said the king, "I understand now the inconstancy of the worlds. I am free of all desire; I am free of the chains of life."

Once again, he paid homage to the Buddha. Then he turned to the servants, assembled in the hall.

"Friends," said he, "I must have wronged you many times, yet never once did you show me that you bore malice. You were kind and good. But before I die, I must have your forgiveness. The wrongs I did you were unintentional; forgive me, friends."

The servants were weeping. They murmured:

"No, you have never wronged us, lord!"

Suddhodana continued:

"And you, Mahaprajapati, you who were my pious consort, you whom I see in tears, calm your grief. My death is a happy death. Think of the glory of this child you brought up; gaze at him in all his splendor, and rejoice."

He died. The sun was setting.

The Master said:

"Behold my father's body. He is no longer what he was. No one has ever conquered death. He who is born must die. Show your zeal for good works; walk in the path that leads to wisdom. Make a lamp of wisdom, and darkness will vanish of its own accord. Do not follow evil laws; do not plant poisonous roots; do not add to the evil in the world.

Like the charioteer who, having left the highroad
for a rough path, weeps at the sight of a broken
axle, even so does the fool, who has strayed from
the law, weep when he falls into the jaws of death.
The wise man is the torch that gives light to the
ignorant; he guides mankind, for he has eyes, and
the others are sightless."

The body was carried to a great funeral pile. The
Master set fire to it, and while his father's body
was being consumed by the flames, while the people of Kapilavastu wept and lamented, he repeated
these sacred truths:

"Suffering is birth, suffering is old age, suffering is sickness, suffering is death. O thirst to be led
from birth to birth! Thirst for power, thirst for
pleasure, thirst for being, thirsts that are the source
of all suffering! O evil thirsts, the saint knows you
not, the saint who extinguishes his desires, the saint
who knows the noble eight-fold path."

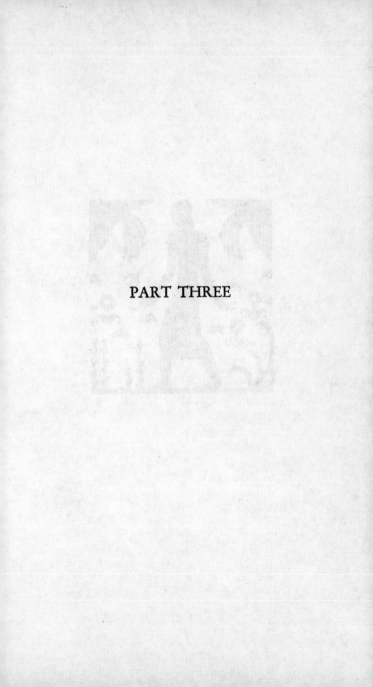

PART THREE

1

MAHAPRAJAPATI was musing. She knew the vanity of this world. She wanted to flee the palace, to flee Kapilavastu, and lead a life of holiness.

"How happy is the Master! How happy are the disciples!" she thought. "Why can I not do as they do? Why can I not live as they live? But they oppose women. We are not admitted to the community, and I must remain in this mournful city, to me deserted; I must remain in this mournful palace, empty in my sight!"

She grieved. She laid aside her costly robes; she gave her jewels to her handmaidens, and she was humble before all creatures.

One day, she said to herself:

"The Master is kind; he will take pity on me. I shall go to him, and perhaps he will be willing to receive me into the community."

The Master was in a wood, near Kapilavastu. Mahaprajapati went to him, and in a timid voice, she said:

"Master, only you and your disciples can be

really happy. Yet I, too, like you and those who accompany you, wish to walk in the path of salvation. May the favor be granted me to enter the community, O Blessed One."

The Master remained silent. She continued:

"How can I be happy in a world I despise? I know its meretricious joys. I long to walk in the path of salvation. May the favor be granted me to enter the community, O Blessed One. And I know many women who are willing to follow me. May the favor be granted us to enter the community, O Blessed One."

The Master still remained silent. She continued:

"My palace is cheerless and dreary. The city is wrapped in darkness. The embroidered veils weigh heavily upon my brow; the diadems, the bracelets and the necklaces hurt me. I must walk in the path of salvation. Many earnest women, many women of great piety, are ready to follow me. May the favor be granted women to enter the community, O Blessed One."

For the third time, the Master remained silent. Mahaprajapati, her eyes full of tears, returned to her gloomy palace.

But she would not accept defeat. She resolved to seek the Master once again and plead with him.

He was then in the great wood, near Vaisali. Mahaprajapati cut off her hair, and putting on a reddish-colored robe made of a coarse material, she set out for Vaisali.

She made the trip on foot; she never once complained of weariness. Covered with dust, she finally arrived at the hall where the Buddha was meditating. But she did not dare to enter; she stood outside the door, with tears in her eyes. Ananda happened to pass by. He saw her and asked:

"O queen, why have you come here, dressed in this manner? Why are you standing before the Master's door?"

"I dare not enter his presence. Three times, already, he has denied my plea, and that which he has thrice refused, I have come to ask him again: that the favor be granted me, that the favor be granted women, to enter the community."

"I shall intercede for you, O queen," said Ananda.

He entered the hall. He saw the Master, and he said to him:

"Blessed One, Mahaprajapati, our revered queen, is standing before your door. She dares not appear before you; she is afraid you will again turn a deaf ear to her plea. Yet it is not the plea of a foolish woman, Blessed One. Would it mean so much to you to grant it? The queen was a mother to you, once; she was always kind to you; surely she deserves to be heard. Why should you not receive women into the community? There are women of great piety, women with the saintly courage to keep in the path of holiness."

"Ananda," said the Master, "do not ask me to permit women to enter the community."

Ananda left. The queen was waiting for him.

"What did the Master say," she asked, anxiously.

"He denies your plea. But do not lose hope."

The following day, Ananda again went to the Blessed One.

"Mahaprajapati has not left the wood," said he. "She is thinking of the happy days of her youth. Maya was then alive; Maya, the most beautiful of all women; Maya, to whom a son would be born. Maya's sister was a noble woman: she knew nothing of envy: she loved this child, even before it came into the world. And when it was born, to bring joy to all creatures, Queen Maya died. Mahaprajapati was kind to the motherless boy: he seemed so frail. She protected him from harm; she gave him devoted nurses; she shielded him from the influence of evil servants; she lavished her care and her tenderness upon him. He grew older, and still she would not leave him. She anticipated his least wishes; she worshipped him. And he attained the happiest fortune; he is the giant tree that shelters the wise; and now, when she would seek a humble place in his shadow, she is refused the peace and rest to which she aspires. O Master, be not unjust; receive Mahaprajapati into the community."

The Master pondered; then he gravely spoke these words:

"Listen, Ananda. Go to Mahaprajapati and tell her that I am willing to receive her into the community, but that she must conform to certain very strict rules. These are the observances I shall require of the women in the community: a nun, even if she has been a nun for a hundred years, must rise in the presence of a monk and show him every mark of deep respect, even though he has been a monk for only a day; the nuns must go to the monks for a public confession of their transgressions and for instruction in the sacred word; nuns guilty of a grave offense must submit to a fitting punishment, for fifteen days, in front of the whole community of monks and nuns; before nuns are admitted to the community, their constancy and their virtue must be tried for a period of two years; the nuns will not be allowed to exhort the monks, but the monks will be allowed to exhort the nuns. These are the observances which, in addition to the observances already known to the monks, will be required of all the nuns."

Mahaprajapati joyfully promised to observe these rules. She entered the community, and within a few months, many women had followed her example.

But, one day, the Master said to Ananda:

"If women had not been admitted to the community, Ananda, chastity would have been preserved a long time, and the true faith would have lived, vigorous and serene, for a thousand years. But now that women are admitted to the community, Ananda, chastity will be in danger, and the true faith, in all its vigor, will live only five hundred years."

FROM Vaisali, the Master went to Cravasti, to Jeta's park. One day, King Prasenajit came to see him.

"My Lord," said the king, "six hermits have recently arrived in Cravasti. They do not believe in your law. They maintain that your knowledge is not equal to theirs, and they have tried to astonish me by performing numerous prodigies. I believe their statements to be untrue, but it would be well, my Lord, if you were to confound their audacity. The world's salvation depends upon your glory. So appear before these cheats and impostors and silence them."

"King," replied the Buddha, "order a great hall to be built near the city. Have it finished in seven days. I shall proceed there. Arrange to have the evil hermits present, and you will then see who performs the greatest prodigies, they or I."

Prasenajit ordered the hall to be built.

While awaiting the day of the trial, the lying hermits sought to delude the Master's faithful followers, and those who refused to listen to their evil

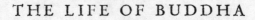

words incurred their bitter enmity. Now, the Master had no truer friend in Cravasti than Prince Kala, a brother of Prasenajit. Kala had shown his utter contempt for the hermits, and they decided to take their revenge.

Kala was a very handsome man. One day, as he was walking through the royal gardens, he met one of Prasenajit's wives, and she playfully threw him a garland of flowers. The hermits heard of the incident, and they told the king that his brother had tried to seduce one of his wives. The king flew into a great rage, and without giving Kala a chance to justify himself, he had his hands and feet cut off.

Poor Kala suffered pitifully. His friends stood around his couch, weeping. One of the evil hermits happened to pass by.

"Come, show your power," they said to him. "You know that Kala is innocent. Make him well again!"

"He believes in the son of the Sakyas," replied the hermit. "It behooves the Sakyas' son to make him well again."

Then Kala began to sing:

"How can the Master of the worlds fail to see my misery? Let us worship the Lord who no longer knows desire; let us adore the Blessed One who takes pity on all creatures."

218

Ananda suddenly appeared before him.

"Kala," said he, "the Master has taught me the words that will heal your wounds."

He recited a few verses, and the prince immediately recovered the use of his limbs.

"Henceforth," he exclaimed, "I shall serve the Master! However humble the tasks which he may assign to me, I shall perform them with joy, to please him."

And he followed Ananda to Jeta's park. The Master received him graciously and admitted him to the community.

The day arrived on which the Master was to compete with the hermits. Early in the morning, King Prasenajit went to the hall he had had built for this occasion. The six hermits were already there. They exchanged glances and smiled.

"King," said one of them, "we are the first to arrive at the place of meeting."

"Do you suppose the one we are expecting will really come?" said another.

"Hermits," said the king, "do not scoff at him. You know how he sent one of his disciples to cure my brother whom I had unjustly punished. He will come. He may even be here, in our midst, without our knowing it."

As the king finished speaking, a luminous cloud filled the hall. It became lighter and lighter; it

219

melted into the daylight, and the Buddha appeared, arrayed in golden splendor. Behind him stood Ananda and Kala. Ananda held a red flower in his hand, Kala a yellow flower, and never, in all the gardens of Cravasti, had any one seen two such flowers as these.

Prasenajit showed his profound admiration. The evil hermits ceased their laughter.

The Blessed One spoke:

"The glowworm shines for all to see, as long as the sun stays hidden, but when the blazing star appears, the poor worm quenches his feeble light. The impostors spoke loudly as long as the Buddha was silent, but now that the Buddha speaks, they weep with fear and are silent."

The hermits were alarmed. They saw the king viewing them with a scornful eye, and they hung their heads in shame.

Suddenly, the roof of the hall disappeared, and on the dome of the sky, stretching from the east to the west, the Master traced a course over which he proceeded to travel. At the sight of this prodigy, his most insolent rival fled in terror. The hermit imagined he was being pursued by a howling pack of hounds, and he never stopped running until he came to the edge of a pool. There, he tied a stone to his neck and threw himself into the water. A fisherman found his body the following day.

In the meanwhile, the Master had created a being in his own image, and, with him, he was now walking in the celestial path. And his great voice was heard, saying:

"O my disciples, I am about to ascend to the abode of the Gods and the Goddesses. Maya, my mother, has summoned me; I must instruct her in the law. I shall remain with her three months. But, each day, I shall descend to earth, and Sariputra, alone, will know where to find me; he will rule the community according to my instructions. And while I am absent from the sky, I shall leave with my mother, to instruct her, this being whom I have created in mine own image."

꒰

AT the end of three months, the Master descended to earth and took the road to Cravasti. As he was approaching Jeta's park, he met a young girl. She was the servant of a wealthy inhabitant of the city who happened to be working in the fields that day. She was taking him a bowl of rice for his meal. At the sight of the Buddha, she felt strangely happy.

"It is the Master, the Blessed One," she thought. "My eyes behold him; my hands could almost touch him, he is so near. Oh, what a holy joy it would be to give him alms! But I have nothing of my own."

She sighed. Her glance fell on the bowl of rice.

"This rice . . . My master's meal . . . No master can reduce to slavery one who is already a slave. Mine could strike me, but what of that! He could put me in chains, but I would bear them lightly. I shall give the rice to the Blessed One."

She presented the bowl to the Buddha. He accepted it and continued on his way to Jeta's park. The young girl, her eyes shining with happiness, went to look for her master.

"Where is my rice?" he asked, as soon as he saw her.

"I gave it to the Buddha as an alms. Punish me if you will, I shall not weep; I am too happy for what I have done."

He did not punish her. He bowed his head and said:

"No, I shall not punish you. I am asleep and your eyes are open. Go; you are no longer a slave."

The young girl made a deep obeisance.

"With your permission then," said she, "I shall go to Jeta's park, and I shall ask the Blessed One to instruct me in the law."

"Go," said the man.

She went to Jeta's park; she sat at the Buddha's feet, and she became one of the most saintly women in the community.

Among those who sought instruction from the Blessed One at the same time as this young slave was Suprabha, the daughter of a prominent citizen of Cravasti. Suprabha was very beautiful. To see her was to fall in love with her, and she was courted by all the distinguished young men of the city. This caused her father no little concern. "To which one shall I give her in marriage?" he would repeatedly ask himself; "those whom I refuse will become my bitter enemies."

And for hours at a time, he would remain deep in thought.

One day, Suprabha said to him:

"You seem to be troubled, dear father. What is the reason?"

"Daughter," he replied, "you alone are the cause of my anxiety. There are so many in Cravasti who wish to marry you!"

"You are afraid to make a choice from among my suitors," said Suprabha. "Poor men! If they but knew my thoughts! Do not be anxious, father! Tell them to assemble, and, according to the ancient custom, I shall go among them, and I myself shall choose a husband from their number."

"I shall do as you wish, daughter."

Suprabha's father went to King Prasenajit and received permission to have a herald proclaim throughout the city:

"That seven days from this day, there will be held an assembly of all the young men who wish to marry Suprabha. The young girl herself will select a husband from among their number."

On the seventh day, a host of suitors gathered in the magnificent garden belonging to Suprabha's father. She appeared, riding in a chariot. She was holding a yellow banner on which was painted the picture of the Blessed One. She was singing his praises. They all looked at her in amazement, and they wondered, "What will she say to us?"

She finally addressed the young men.

"I can not love any of you," said she, "but do not think that I spurn you. Love is not my aim in life; I want to take refuge with the Buddha. I shall go to the park where he dwells, and he will instruct me in the law."

Mournfully, the young men withdrew, and Suprabha went to Jeta's park. She heard the Blessed One speak; she was admitted to the community, and she became a most devoted nun.

One day, as she was leaving the sacred gardens, she was recognized by one of her former suitors who happened to be passing with several friends.

"We must carry off this woman," said he. "I loved her once; I still love her. She shall be mine."

His friends agreed to help him. Before Suprabha was aware of it, she was surrounded, and they suddenly rushed upon her. But as they were about to seize her, she directed her thought toward the Buddha, and, immediately, she rose in the air. A crowd gathered; Suprabha soared above them for a while, then, flying with the grace and majesty of a swan, she returned to her sacred dwelling.

And their cries followed her:

"O saintly one, you make manifest the power

of the faithful; O saint, you render manifest the power of the Buddha. It would be unjust to condemn you to the earthly pleasures of love, O saintly one, O saint."

卐

KING Prasenajit had a daughter named Virupa. She had reached a marriageable age. Unfortunately, she was extremely ugly; no prince or warrior would have her for a wife, and even the merchants looked at her askance.

But presently a wealthy stranger came to live in Cravasti. His name was Ganga. The king thought, "Ganga has never seen my daughter. Perhaps he will not refuse to marry her." And he summoned him to the palace.

Ganga was highly flattered by Prasenajit's offer. He was of humble birth, and although, as a merchant, he had amassed a great fortune, he had never dreamed of marrying a princess. He therefore accepted the proposal.

"Then come to the palace this very evening," said the king, "and take my daughter home with you."

He obeyed. The night was dark, and the wedding took place without Ganga having seen his betrothed. Then Virupa accompanied her husband to his home.

Ganga saw his wife the next day. Her ugliness frightened him. He wanted to turn her out of the house, but he did not dare; he feared the king's vengeance. He kept her at home, but she was virtually a prisoner; she was not allowed to go out, for any reason whatsoever.

She was very unhappy. In vain she gave her husband constant proof of her affection; he only showed his aversion and his contempt for her. He never looked at her. He hardly spoke to her. And Virupa felt lonely and forlorn.

One day, Ganga was invited to a feast given by some of his friends. "Whoever comes without wife," he was warned, "will be fined five hundred pieces of gold."

Ganga decided to attend; it would relieve the monotony of his existence. But he did not want to show Virupa to his friends; he was afraid of being ridiculed. "I shall pay the five hundred pieces of gold," he thought, "and they will not make fun of me."

That day, Virupa was sadder than usual. She knew where her husband had gone, and she wept. She said to herself:

"What good is a life as dreary as mine? I never have any pleasure. My master loathes me. And I can not blame him; I am ugly; every one has told me so. I have brought joy to no one. Oh, I loathe myself. Death would be better than this life I lead; death would be sweet. I shall kill myself."

She took a rope and hung herself.

At that same moment, in Jeta's park, the Master was wondering, "Who is suffering to-day in Cravasti? Whom can I save from misery? To what unfortunate being can I lend a helping hand?"

By his power of divination, he learned of Virupa's distress. He flew to Ganga's house; he entered. Virupa was still alive. The Master loosened the rope she had fastened about her neck. She breathed deeply and looked around. She recognized the Master. She fell at his feet and made him a pious offering. Then he said:

"Look at yourself in a mirror, Virupa."

She obeyed. She uttered a cry of joy and astonishment. She was as beautiful as a daughter of the Gods. Again she wanted to worship the Buddha, but he had disappeared.

In the meanwhile, Ganga had not been spared the banter of his friends.

"Why did you come without your wife?" they asked him. "Are you afraid to let us see her? She must be very beautiful. You jealous husband!"

Ganga was at a loss for an answer. The feast bored him. One of his friends handed him a cup of intoxicating wine.

"Drink, Ganga," said he. "We laugh, and you

229

are almost in tears. Come, laugh with us. Drink; this wine will teach you to laugh."

Ganga took the cup. He drank. He became livelier. He drank again. Presently, he was drunk. And he kept on drinking until, finally, he fell into a heavy sleep.

"Let us hurry over to his house, while he is asleep," said his friends. "We shall see his wife, and we shall find out why he keeps her out of sight."

They entered Ganga's home. Virupa had the mirror in her hand; she was looking at herself. Her eyes were bright with happiness. All the guests admired her, and they went away, quietly, saying, "We now understand Ganga's jealousy."

Ganga was still sleeping. They awoke him and said:

"Great is your felicity, friend. What did you do that was so pleasing to the Gods, to deserve a wife of such rare beauty?"

"This is too much!" cried Ganga. "What have I ever done to you that you should insult me so cruelly?"

And he abruptly left them. He was raging with anger and mortification. He flung open the door of his house; he strode through the halls, muttering imprecations; but, suddenly, the curses died upon his lips. He turned pale with astonishment. Before him was standing a woman of incomparable beauty. She was smiling. He slowly came to his senses; then he, too, smiled, and he asked:

"O you who appear before me like some radiant Goddess new-risen from her bed of flowers, O well-beloved, who made you so beautiful?"

Virupa told him the story. From that day, she and her husband knew true happiness, and they both sought every opportunity to evince their faith in the Buddha and show him their gratitude.

IN the meanwhile, the evil hermits, whose imposture the Buddha had exposed, were being treated with contempt by the populace, and each day their desire for vengeance grew more intense. They had established themselves near Jeta's park, and night and day they spied upon the Buddha and his disciples. But all in vain; they saw nothing that gave them the slightest excuse for slandering the community.

At last, one of the hermits said to his companions:

"We have long been observing the conduct of these monks. Their virtue can not be denied. Still, we must turn the minds of the people against them, and I think I have found a way. I know a young girl of great charm. Her name is Sinca. She is very clever at practising deceit. She will not refuse to help us, and soon the glory of this Sakya will vanish."

The hermits sent word to Sinca. She came.

"Why did you send for me?" she asked.

"Do you know the monk from Kapilavastu, the one who is worshipped as the Buddha?"

"No, but I know of his great fame. I have been told of the many prodigies he has performed."

"This man is our bitterest enemy, Sinca. He treats us shamefully and would destroy our power. Now, you believe in us; come, take our part. She who will have conquered the conqueror may well be proud; she will be famous among women, and the world will ring with her praises."

Sinca was carried away by the hermit's words. She assured him that the Buddha would soon be disgraced and his name hated throughout the earth.

Each day, now, she went to Jeta's park, at a time when those who had been listening to the Master preach were beginning to leave. She was dressed in flaming red, and she carried flowers in her arms. And if, by chance, some one asked her, "Where are you going?" she would reply, "What business is it of yours?" When she came to the park, she waited until she was quite alone; then, instead of entering the Buddha's domain, she set out for the dwelling of the evil hermits. There, she spent the night, but at dawn she returned to the gates of the park, and when she was sure to be seen by the early risers on their way to their devotions, she would leave and return home. And to those who asked, "Where do you come from, so early in the morning?" she would reply, "What business is it of yours?"

At the end of one month, she gave a different

answer. In the evening she would say, "I am going to Jeta's park, where the Blessed One is waiting for me," and in the morning, "I have just come from Jeta's park, where I spent the night with the Blessed One." And there were some poor, credulous people who believed her and who suspected the Master of unchastity.

The sixth month, she took a piece of cloth and wrapped it around her body. "She is pregnant," they thought, and the fools maintained that the Master's virtue was only a pretense.

When the ninth month arrived, she tied a wooden ball to the thick girdle about her waist, and when she walked, she assumed a languorous gait. Finally, one night, she entered the hall where the Master was expounding the law. Boldly, she faced him, and her strident voice interrupted his speech.

"Sweet is your voice and honeyed your words as you instruct the people in the law. While I, who am pregnant because of you, I, who am soon to become a mother, have not even a place for my confinement! You would deny me the very oil and butter I need. If it would make you blush, now, to look after me, you could at least entrust me to one of your disciples, or to King Prasenajit, or to the merchant Anathapindika. But no! I am nothing to you any more, and little you care about the child that will be born! You would know all the joys of love, but the responsibilities you would ignore!"

"Is that a lie or are you telling the truth, Sinca?" asked the Master, calmly. "Only you and I know."

"You know very well I am not lying," cried Sinca.

The Master retained his composure. But Indra, who had been watching from the sky, decided it was time to expose Sinca's impudence. He had four Gods take the form of mice. They crawled under her robe and gnawed at the string that was holding the wooden ball. The ball fell to the ground.

"There, your child is born," exclaimed the Master with a laugh.

The disciples turned upon Sinca in their rage. They reviled her; they spat in her face; they beat her. She fled. She was weeping with pain and shame and anger. Suddenly, red flames sprang up around her and enveloped her in a mantle of fire, and she, who had dared to slander the Buddha, came to a cruel and terrible end.

6

THE Master left Jeta's park. He stopped in the cities and in the villages to preach the law, and full many there were to adopt the true faith.

One day, an old man and his wife invited the Master to take his meal with them.

"My Lord," said the old man, "we have long been eager to hear your word. We are happy, now that we know the sacred truths, and among your friends you will find none more devout than we."

"I am not surprised," replied the Buddha, "for you and I were near relations in our former existences."

"Master," said the woman, "my husband and I have lived together since our early youth; we have now attained a ripe old age. Life has been kind to us. Never has the slightest quarrel come between us. We still love each other as in the days gone by, and the evening of our lives is as sweet as was the dawn. May it be granted us, my Lord, to love each other in our next existence as we have loved one another in this life."

"It will be granted," said the Master; "the Gods have protected you!"

He continued on his way. He saw an old woman drawing water from a well by the side of the road. He approached her.

"I am thirsty," said he. "Will you give me a drink?"

The old woman stared at him. She was deeply moved. She began to weep. She wanted to embrace the Master, but she was afraid. The tears coursed down her cheeks.

"Embrace me," said the Master.

The old woman ran to his arms, and she murmured:

"Now I can die happy. I have seen the Blessed One, and it was given me to embrace him."

He went on. He came to a vast forest where a herd of buffaloes lived with their keepers. One of these buffaloes was a very powerful animal. He had an ugly temper. He barely tolerated the presence of his keepers, and at the approach of a stranger he would become aggressive. When the stranger came near, he would attack him with his horns, and he would often wound him seriously. Sometimes he killed him.

The keepers saw the Blessed One walking along, quietly, and they shouted:

"Take care, traveller. Do not come near us. There is a vicious buffalo here."

But he paid no attention to the warning. He made straight for the spot where the buffalo was grazing.

All at once, the buffalo raised his head and sniffed noisily; then, lowering his horns, he rushed at the Master. The keepers trembled. "Our voices were not loud enough," they cried; "he did not hear us." But, suddenly, the animal stopped short; he knelt before the Master and began licking his feet. There was a look of pleading in his eyes.

The Master gently stroked the buffalo. He spoke to him in a quiet voice.

"Say to yourself that all earthly things are transitory, that peace is found only in nirvana. Do not weep. Believe in me, believe in my goodness, in my compassion, and your condition will change. You will not be reborn among the animals, and, in time, you will attain the sky and dwell among the Gods."

From that day, the buffalo was extremely docile. And the keepers, who had expressed their admiration for the Master and who had given him what alms they could afford, were instructed in the law, and they became known for their piety, even among the most pious.

7

THE Master arrived at the city of Kausambi, and there, at first, he was very happy. The inhabitants eagerly listened to his words, and many of them became monks. King Udayana was among the believers, and he allowed his son Rashtrapala to enter the community.

Yet it was in Kausambi that the Master met with one of his great sorrows. A monk, one day, was reprimanded for committing some minor offense. He would not own himself in the wrong; so he was punished. He refused to submit to the punishment, and, as he was a pleasant man, of great wit and learning, there were many to take his part. In vain the others besought him to return to the straight path.

"Do not assume that conceited air," they said to him; "do not consider yourself incapable of making mistakes. Heed our wise advice. Address the other monks as they should be addressed who profess a faith that is also yours; they will address you as he should be addressed who professes a faith that is also theirs. The community will grow, the community will flourish, only if the monks will take counsel from one another."

"It is not for you to tell me what is right or wrong," he replied. "Stop reproving me."

"Do not say that. Your words offend against the law. You are defying discipline; you are sowing discord in the community. Come, mend your ways. Live at peace with the community. Avoid these quarrels, and be faithful to the law."

It was useless. They then decided to expel the rebel, but, once again, he refused to obey. He would remain in the community: since he was innocent, there was no need to submit to an unjust punishment.

The Master finally intervened. He tried to pacify the monks; he pleaded with them to forget their grievances and to unite, as before, in the performance of their sacred duties, but no one paid any attention. And, one day, a monk even had the audacity to say to him:

"Keep still, O Master; do not bother us with your speeches. You have arrived at a knowledge of the law; meditate upon it. You will find your meditations quite delightful. As for us, we shall know where to go; our quarrels will not keep us from finding the way. Meditate, and be quiet."

The Master was not angry. He tried to speak, but it was impossible, He saw then that he could never convince the monks of Kausambi; they seemed to be possessed with some sudden folly. The Master decided to forsake them, but first he said to them:

"Happy is he who has a faithful friend; happy is he who has a discerning friend. What obstacles could two wise and virtuous friends not overcome? But he who has no faithful friend resembles a king without a country: he must roam in solitude, like the elephant in the wild forest. Yet it is better to travel alone than in the company of a fool. The wise man should follow a lonely path; he should avoid evil and should preserve his serenity, like the elephant in the wild forest."

He left. No one tried to stop him. He went to a village where he knew he would find his disciple Bhrigu. Bhrigu was overjoyed to see him, and the Master was not a little comforted. Then, Anuruddha, Nanda and Kimbala joined him. They gave him every proof of their respect and friendship, and they lived at peace with one another. And the Master thought, "So there are some, among my disciples, who love me and who do not quarrel."

One day, as he sat down in the shade of a tree and began thinking of the troublous times in Kausambi, a herd of elephants stopped to rest not far from him. The biggest elephant went down to the river and drew water which he brought back to the others. They drank; then, instead of thanking

him for doing them this service, they abused him,
they beat him with their trunks, and, finally, they
drove him away. And the Master saw that his own
experience was not unlike that of the elephant:
they were both victims of gross ingratitude. The
elephant noticed the sadness in his face; he drew
near and looked at him tenderly; then left, to go in
search of food and drink for him.

The Master finally returned to Cravasti and
rested in Jeta's park.

But it still grieved him to think of the cruel
monks of Kausambi. One morning, however, he
saw them enter the park. They were in great distress: alms had been denied them, for every one
was indignant at their treatment of the Master.
They had come to beg his forgiveness. The guilty
monk confessed himself to have been in the wrong,
and his punishment was light. His adversaries, as
well as his friends, admitted the error of their ways,
and all promised strictly to obey the rules. And
the Master was happy: there was no longer any
dissension in the community.

8

ONE day, he returned to the country of Rajagriha.

In a field, not far from the city, he came upon a brahman named Bharadvaja. It was the harvest season, and the brahman and his servants were joyously celebrating. They were laughing and singing as the Master went by. He held out his alms-bowl, and those who recognized him, greeted him and made him many friendly offerings. This displeased Bharadvaja. He went up to the Master, and he said to him in a loud voice:

"Monk, tarry not in our midst; you set an evil example. We work, we that are here, and with watchful eyes, we observe the changes of seasons. When it is time to plow, my servants plow; when it is time to sow, they sow; and I plow and sow with them. Then the day comes when we harvest the fruit of our labor. We provide our own food, and when it is stored away, we have good reason to rest and play. While you, you roam the streets and walk the roads, and the only trouble you deign to take is to hold out a bowl to those you meet. It would be better far for you to work; it would be better far to plow and sow."

The Master smiled and answered:

"Friend, like you I plow and sow, and when my work is done, I eat."

"You plow? You sow?" said Bharadvaja. "How can I believe that? Where are your cattle? Where is your grain? Where is your plow?"

The Master said:

"Purity of understanding, that is the glorious seed I sow. Works of holiness are the rain that falls upon the fertile earth where the seed sprouts and ripens. And mine is a mighty plow: it has wisdom for its plowshare, the law for its handles, and an active faith is the powerful bullock yoked to its pole. Desire is uprooted like weeds in the fields I plow, and I gather in the richest of harvests, nirvana."

He continued on his way. But the brahman Bharadvaja followed him; he would now hear the sacred word.

They entered the city. On the public square, a large crowd was watching a troop of dancers. The daughter of the leader was attracting particular attention. Such grace and beauty had seldom been seen, and, whenever she appeared, those who were not master of their passions burned with the desire to possess her. Her name was Kuvalaya.

She had just finished dancing. Ardent eyes were still fastened upon her. She was aware of her power, and full of pride and audacity, she shouted to the crowd:

"Admire me, my lords! In all Rajagriha is there one who can surpass Kuvalaya in beauty, are there any who can even equal her?"

"Yes, woman," replied the brahman Bharadvaja. "What is your beauty when compared with the beauty of the Master?"

"I would see this Master whose beauty you praise," said Kuvalaya; "lead me to him."

"Here he is," said the Blessed One.

And he came forward.

The dancer stared at him.

"You are beautiful," she said at last. "I shall dance for you."

Kuvalaya danced. The dance began slowly. She had wrapped all her veils about her, even covering her face, and the beauty once so boldly flaunted was now only a dim promise. She was like the moon, hiding behind soft clouds from the gaze of night. A cloud flew away; a faint ray escaped through the rift. The dance became more rapid; one by one the veils fell away, and the queen of the stars appeared in all her glory. Faster and faster she

245

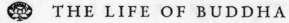

whirled; suddenly, a blinding light flashed in her eyes, and she stopped. She was naked. The crowd gasped and surged forward.

"Unhappy woman!" said the Buddha.

He looked at her intently. Whereupon Kuvalaya's cheeks became sunken, her forehead wrinkled and her eyes grew dull. Only a few ugly teeth were left in her mouth; only a few thin strands of grey hair still hung from her head, and she was stooped as with age. The Blessed One had punished her as he had once punished Mara's daughters when they had tried to tempt him; he had changed the beautiful dancer into a shrivelled old woman.

She sighed:

"Master, I know the great wrong I have done. An ephemeral beauty had made me vain. You taught me a bitter lesson, but I feel that some day I shall be happy to have received it. Let me learn the sacred truths; then may I be released for ever from this body that, even when it was the delight of men, was nothing but a loathsome corpse."

The Master granted Kuvalaya's request, and she became one of the most devout of the Buddha's faithful followers.

9

IN the city of Atavi there ruled a king who was
very fond of hunting. One day, he saw an
enormous deer and started in pursuit. The
deer was fleet of foot, and in the heat of the chase,
the king lost sight of the other hunters. Finally, the
prey escaped, and weary and discouraged, the king
sat down under a tree. He fell asleep.

It happened that a wicked God named Alavaka
lived in the tree. He liked to feed on human flesh,
and he killed and devoured all who came near him.
He saw the king; he rejoiced, and the poor hunter
was about to be dealt a severe blow when a noise
fortunately awoke him. He realized that his life
was threatened; he made an attempt to rise, but the
God took him by the throat and held him down.
Then the king tried to plead with him.

"Spare me, my lord!" said he. "By your terrifying appearance, I know you to be one of the
Gods that eat human flesh. Oh, deign to be kind to
me. You will have no cause to regret your mercy. I
shall reward you with magnificent gifts."

"What care I for gifts!" replied Alavaka. "It

is your flesh I want; it will appease my hunger."

"My lord," replied the king, "if you let me return to Atavi, I shall send you a man every day to satisfy your hunger."

"When you get back to your home, you will forget this promise."

"No," said the king, "I never forget a promise. Besides, if I should once fail to make this daily offering, you have only to come to my palace and tell me of your grievance, and, immediately, without resisting, I shall follow you, and you may devour me."

The God allowed himself to be persuaded, and the king returned to the city of Atavi. But he kept thinking of his cruel promise; there was no way he could evade it, and henceforth he would have to be a hard and ruthless master.

He sent for his minister and told him what had happened. The minister considered for a moment, then said to the king:

"My lord, in the prison of Atavi there are criminals who have been condemned to death. We can send them to the God. When he sees that you are keeping faith with him, perhaps he will relieve you of your promise."

The king approved of the suggestion. Guards were sent to the prison, and to those whose days were numbered they said:

"Not far from the city there is a tree inhabited by a God who is very fond of rice. Whoever leaves a plate of rice for him at the foot of the tree will be granted a full pardon."

Whereupon, each day, one of these men, carrying a plate of rice, joyously set out for the tree, never to return.

Presently, there were no men condemned to death left in prison. The minister ordered the judges to be extremely severe and to acquit no one accused of murder except on irrefutable proof of his innocence, but it was in vain; some new way had to be found for appeasing the hunger of the God. Then they began to sacrifice the thieves.

In spite of all their efforts to apprehend the guilty, the prison was again empty, and the king and his minister were compelled to look for victims among the worthy inhabitants of the city. Old people were carried off and forcibly led to the tree, and if the guards were not fleet-footed, the God would sometimes devour them and the victims as well.

A vague uneasiness possessed the city of Atavi. The old people were seen to disappear; no one knew what became of them. And, each day, the king's remorse grew more poignant. But he lacked the courage to sacrifice his life to the welfare of his people. He thought:

"Will no one come to my assistance? There lives in Cravasti, and sometimes in Rajagriha, I have been told, a man of great power, a Buddha, whose prodigies are loudly praised. They say he is fond of travelling. Why, then, does he not come into my kingdom?"

By his power of divination, the Buddha knew of the king's desire. He flew through the air and came to Alavaka's tree. There, he sat down.

The God saw him. He started walking toward him, but, suddenly, he became powerless. His knees trembled. Fury seized him.

"Who are you?" he asked, fiercely.

"A being far more powerful than yourself," replied the Buddha.

Alavaka was in a terrible rage. He would have liked to torture this man who was sitting on the ground in front of him, this man whom he could not reach; he would have liked to torture him to death. The Buddha never lost his composure.

Alavaka finally managed to control himself. He thought that cunning would perhaps succeed where strength had failed, and in a pleasant voice he said:

"I see you are a wise man, my Lord; it is always a pleasure for me to interrogate men of wisdom. I ask them four questions. If they can answer, they are free to go wherever they please; if they can not answer, they remain my prisoners, and I devour them when I feel so disposed."

"Ask me the four questions," said the Buddha.

"I must warn you," said Alavaka, "that no one has ever answered them. You will find scattered around the bones of those I interrogated in the past."

"Ask me the four questions," repeated the Buddha.

"Well then," said Alavaka, "how can man avoid the river of passions? How can he cross the sea of existences and find safe harbor? How can he escape the tempests of evil? How can he be left untouched by the storm of desires?"

In a quiet voice, the Buddha replied:

"Man avoids the river of passions if he believes in the Buddha, in the law and in the community; he crosses the sea of existences and finds safe harbor if he understands works of holiness; he will escape the tempests of evil if he performs works of holiness; he will be left untouched by the storm of desires if he knows the sacred path that leads to deliverance."

When Alavaka heard the Master's answers, he fell at his feet and worshipped him, and he promised to change his savage ways. Then, together, they went to Atavi, to the palace of the king.

"King," said the God, "I release you from your pledge."

THE LIFE OF BUDDHA

The king was happier than he had ever been before. When he knew who had saved him, he cried:
"I believe in you, my Lord, who have saved me
and saved my people; I believe in you, and I shall
dedicate my life to proclaiming your glory, the
glory of the law and the glory of the community."

10

THE monk Devadatta was possessed of an arrogant nature. He was impatient of any restraint. He aspired to supplant the Buddha, but the monks, he knew, would not join him in an open revolt. For that he needed the support of some king or prince.

"King Vimbasara is an old man," he said to himself, one day; "Prince Ajatasatru, who is young and brave, is eager to succeed him to the throne. I could advise the prince to his advantage, and, in return, he could help me to become the head of the community."

He went to see Ajatasatru. He addressed him in flattering terms; he praised his strength, his courage, his beauty.

"Oh, if you were king," said he, "what glory would come to Rajagriha! You would conquer the neighboring states; all the sovereigns of the world would pay you homage: you would be the omnipotent master, and you would be worshipped like a God."

With such words as these, Devadatta won Ajatasatru's confidence. He received many precious gifts, and he became still more arrogant.

Maudgalyayana noticed Devadatta's frequent visits to the prince. He decided to warn the Blessed One.

"My Lord," he began, "Devadatta is very friendly with Prince Ajatasatru."

The Blessed One interrupted him.

"Let Devadatta do as he pleases; we shall soon know the truth. I am aware that Ajatasatru pays him homage; it does not advance him a single step in the path of virtue. Let Devadatta glory in his arrogance! It will be his ruin. As the banana-tree and the bamboo-tree bear fruit only to die, so will the honors Devadatta is receiving simply hasten his downfall."

Devadatta soon reached the height of vanity. He could not abide the Buddha's grandeur, and, one day, he made bold to say to him:

"Master, you are now well along in years; it is a great hardship for you to rule the monks; you should retire. Meditate in peace upon the sublime law you have discovered, and the community let me take charge of."

The Master smiled quizzically.

"Be not concerned about me, Devadatta; you are too kind. I shall know when it is time to retire. For the present, I shall stay in charge of the community. Besides, when the time does come, I shall not give it even to Sariputra or Maudgalyayana, those two great minds that are like blazing torches, and you want it, Devadatta, you who have such a mediocre intelligence, you who shed even less light than a night-lamp!"

Devadatta bowed respectfully before the Master, but he could not hide the fire of anger in his eyes.

The Master then sent for learned Sariputra.

"Sariputra," said he, "go through the city of Rajagriha and cry in a loud voice: 'Beware of Devadatta! He has strayed from the path of righteousness. The Buddha is not responsible for his words or for his actions; the law no longer inspires him, the community no longer interests him. Henceforth, Devadatta speaks only for himself.' "

It grieved Sariputra to have such a painful mission to perform; however, he understood the Master's reasons, and he went through the city crying Devadatta's shame. The inhabitants stopped to listen, and some thought, "The monks envy Devadatta his friendship for Prince Ajatasatru." But the others said, "Devadatta must have committed a serious offense, for the Blessed One thus publicly to denounce him."

11

DEVADATTA was musing:
"Siddhartha thought to humiliate me by making light of my intelligence. I shall show him he is mistaken. My glory will overshadow his: the night-lamp will become the sun. But King Vimbasara is his faithful friend; he protects him. As long as the king is living, I can do nothing. Prince Ajatasatru, on the other hand, honors me and holds me in high esteem; he reposes implicit confidence in me. If he were to reign, I would get everything I desire."

He went to Ajatasatru's palace.

"Oh, prince," said he, "we are living in an unfortunate age! They that are best fitted to govern are likely to die without ever having reigned. Human life is so brief a thing! Your father's longevity causes me no little concern for you."

He kept on talking, and he was presently giving the prince most evil advice. The prince was weak; he listened. Before long, he had decided to kill his father."

Night and day, now, Ajatasatru wandered

through the palace, watching for an opportunity to slip into his father's apartments and make away with him. But he could not escape the vigilance of the guards. His restlessness puzzled them, and they said to King Vimbasara:

"O king, your son Ajatasatru has been behaving strangely of late. Could he be planning an evil deed?"

"Be silent," replied the king. "My son is a man of noble character. It would not occur to him to do anything base."

"You ought to send for him, O king, and question him."

"Be silent, guards. Do not accuse my son lightly."

The guards continued to keep a close watch, and at the end of a few days, they again spoke to the king. To convince them that they were mistaken, the king summoned Ajatasatru.

The prince appeared before his father. He was trembling.

"My lord," said he, "why did you send for me?"

"Son," said Vimbasara, "my guards say that you have been behaving strangely of late. They tell me you wander through the palace, acting mysteriously, and that you shun the gaze of those you meet. Son, are they not lying?"

"They are not lying, father," said Ajatasatru.

Remorse suddenly overwhelmed him. He fell at the king's feet, and out of the depths of his shame, he cried:

"Father, I wanted to kill you."

Vimbasara shuddered. In a voice full of anguish, he asked:

"Why did you want to kill me?"

"In order to reign."

"Then reign," cried the king. "Royalty is not worth a son's enmity."

Ajatasatru was proclaimed king the next day.

The first thing he did was to have great honors paid to his father. But Devadatta still feared the old king's authority; he decided to use his influence against him.

"As long as your father is allowed his freedom," he said to Ajatasatru, "you are in danger of losing your power. He still retains many followers; you must take measures to intimidate them."

Devadatta again was able to impose his will on Ajatasatru, and poor Vimbasara was thrown into prison. Ajatasatru presently decided to starve him to death, and he allowed no one to take him any food.

But Queen Vaidehi was sometimes permitted to visit Vimbasara in his prison, and she would take rice to him which he ate ravenously. Ajatasatru, however, soon put a stop to this; he ordered the

guards to search her each time she went to see the
prisoner. She then tried to hide the food in her
hair, and when this, too, was discovered, she had
to use great ingenuity to save the king from dying
of hunger. But she was repeatedly found out, and
Ajatasatru, finally, denied her access to the prison.

In the meanwhile, he was persecuting the Buddha's faithful followers. They were forbidden
to look after the temple where Vimbasara, formerly, had placed a lock of the Master's hair and
the parings of his finger-nails. No longer were
flowers or perfume left there as pious offerings, and
the temple was not even cleaned or swept.

In Ajatasatru's palace there dwelt a woman
named Srimati. She was very devout. It grieved her
to be unable to perform works of holiness, and she
wondered how, in these sad times, she could prove
to the Master that she had kept her faith. Passing
in front of the temple, she complained bitterly to
see it so deserted, and when she noticed how un-
clean it was, she wept.

"The Master shall know that there is still one
woman in this house who would honor him,"
thought Srimati, and at the risk of her life, she
swept out the temple and decorated it with a bright
garland.

Ajatasatru saw the garland. He was greatly in-
censed and wanted to know who had dared to dis-

obey him. Srimati did not try to hide; of her own accord, she appeared before the king.

"Why did you defy my orders?" asked Ajatasatru.

"If I defied your orders," she replied, "I respected those of your father, King Vimbasara."

Ajatasatru did not wait to hear further. Pale with fury, he rushed at Srimati and stabbed her with his dagger. She fell, mortally wounded; but her eyes were shining with joy, and in a happy voice, she sang:

"My eyes have seen the protector of the worlds; my eyes have seen the light of the worlds, and for him, in the night, I have lighted the lamps. For him who dissipates the darkness, I have dissipated the darkness. His brilliance is greater than the brilliance of the sun; his rays are purer than the rays of the sun, and my rapt gaze is dazzled by the splendor. For him who dissipates the darkness, I have dissipated the darkness."

And, dead, she seemed to glow with the light of sanctity.

12

DEVADATTA was eager to succeed the Buddha as head of the community. One day, he said to King Ajatasatru:

"My lord, the Buddha holds you in contempt. He hates you. You must put him to death, for your glory is at stake. Send some men to the Bamboo Grove with orders to kill him; I shall lead the way."

Ajatasatru was easily persuaded. The assassins came to the Bamboo Grove, but when they saw the Master, they fell at his feet and worshipped him. This added fuel to Devadatta's rage. He went to the royal stables where a savage elephant was kept, and he bribed the guards to release him when the Master passed by, so that the animal could gore him with his tusks or trample him underfoot. But at the sight of the Master, the elephant became quite gentle, and going up to him, with his trunk he brushed the dust from the sacred robes. And the Master smiled and said:

"This is the second time, thanks to Devadatta, that an elephant has paid homage to me."

Then Devadatta himself tried to do harm to the Master. He saw him meditating in the shade of a tree, and he had the audacity to throw a sharp stone at him. It struck him in the foot; the wound began to bleed. The Master said:

"You have committed a serious offense, Devadatta; the punishment will be terrible. Vain are your criminal attempts upon the life of the Blessed One; he will not meet with an untimely death. The Blessed One will pass away of his own accord, and at the hour he chooses."

Devadatta fled. He decided he would no longer obey the rules of the community, and, wherever he could, he would seek followers of his own.

In the meanwhile, Vimbasara was starving. But he did not die. A mysterious force sustained him. His son finally decided to have him put to death, and he gave orders to burn the soles of his feet, to slash his limbs and to pour boiling oil and salt on the open wounds. The executioner obeyed, and even he wept to see an old man tortured.

A son was born to Ajatasatru on the day he issued the order for his father's death. When he saw the child, a great joy came to him; he relented, and he hurriedly sent guards to the prison to stop the execution. But they arrived too late; King Vimbasara had died amid frightful suffering.

Then Ajatasatru began to repent. One day, he heard Queen Vaidehi saying to the infant prince, as she carried him in her arms:

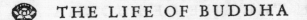

"May your father be as kind to you as his father was to him. Once, when he was a child, he had a sore on his finger; it hurt him, and he cried; no ointment would heal it; so Vimbasara put the finger to his lips and drew out the pus, and Ajatasatru was able to laugh again and play. Oh, love your father, little child; do not punish him with your cruelty for having been cruel to Vimbasara."

Ajatasatru shed bitter tears. He was overwhelmed with remorse. At night, in his dreams, he saw his father, bleeding from his wounds, and he heard him moan. He was seized with a burning fever, and the physician Jivaka was summoned to attend him.

"I can do nothing for you," said Jivaka. "Your body is not sick. Go to the Perfect Master, the Blessed One, the Buddha; he alone knows the words of consolation that will restore you to health."

Ajatasatru took Jivaka's advice. He went to the Blessed One; he confessed his misdeeds and his crimes, and he found peace.

"Your father," the Buddha said to him, "has been reborn among the most powerful Gods; he knows of your repentance, and he forgives you. Heed me, King Ajatasatru; know the law, and cease to suffer."

Ajatasatru issued a proclamation, banishing Devadatta from the kingdom, and ordering the inhabitants to close their doors to him if he were to seek refuge in their homes.

Devadatta was then near Cravasti where he hoped to be received by King Prasenajit, but he was scornfully denied an audience and was told to leave the kingdom. Thwarted in his attempts to enlist followers, he finally set out for Kapilavastu.

He entered the city as night was falling. The streets were dark, almost deserted; no one recognized him as he passed, for how could this lean, wretched monk, slinking in the shadow of the walls, be identified with the proud Devadatta? He went straight to the palace where princess Gopa dwelt in solitude.

He was admitted to her presence.

"Monk," said Gopa, "why do you wish to see me? Do you bring me a message of happiness? Do you come with orders from a husband I deeply reverence?"

"Your husband! Little he cares about you! Think of the time he wickedly deserted you!"

"He deserted me for the world's salvation."

"Do you still love him?"

"My love would defile the purity of his life."

"Then hate him with all your heart."

"With all my heart I respect him."

"Woman, he spurned you; take your revenge."

"Be quiet, monk. Your words are evil."

"Do you not recognize me? I am Devadatta, who loves you."

"Devadatta, Devadatta, I knew you were false and evil; I knew you would be a faithless monk, but I never suspected the depths of your villainy."

"Gopa, Gopa, I love you! Your husband scorned you, he was cruel. Take your revenge. Love me!"

Gopa blushed. From her gentle eyes fell tears of shame.

"It is you who scorn me! Your love would be an insult if it were sincere, but you lie when you say you love me. You seldom noticed me in the days when I was young, in the days when I was beautiful! And now that you see me, an old woman, worn out by my austere duties, you tell me of your love, of your guilty love! You are the most contemptible of men, Devadatta! Go away! Go away!"

In his rage he sprang at her. She put out her hand to protect herself, and he fell to the ground. As he rolled over, blood gushed from his mouth.

He fled. The Sakyas heard that he was in Kapilavastu; they made him leave the city under an escort of guards, and he was taken to the Buddha who was to decide his fate. He pretended to be repentant, but he had dipped his nails in a deadly poison, and as he lay prostrate before the Maser, he tried to scratch his ankle. The Master pushed him away with his toe; then the ground opened; fierce flames burst forth, and they swallowed up the infamous Devadatta.

13

ALTHOUGH the Buddha had chastened Ajatasatru's spirit, there were times when the king still gave way to anger. One day, because of a quarrel between a man from Rajagriha and one from Cravasti, he declared war on King Prasenajit.

He collected a vast army. There were foot-soldiers and horsemen; there were some mounted on chariots, others enclosed in towers carried by elephants, and swords and lances flashed in the sun as they marched into battle.

King Prasenajit also assembled his troops. He too had chariots and horses and elephants, and he advanced to meet Ajatasatru.

It was a terrible battle. It lasted four days. The first day Prasenajit lost his elephants; the second day he lost his horses; on the third, his chariots were destroyed; and on the fourth, his foot-soldiers were killed or made prisoners; and Prasenajit himself, defeated and panic-stricken, fled in the only chariot that had been saved in the disaster and escaped to Cravasti.

There, in a small, unlighted hall, he flung himself down on a low couch. He was silent, a prey to his melancholy thoughts. He never stirred; he appeared to be dead, except for the tears that coursed down his cheeks.

A man entered; it was the merchant Anathapindika.

"My lord," said he, "long may you live, and may the tide of victory turn!"

"My soldiers are dead," the king lamented, "all my soldiers are dead! My soldiers! My soldiers!"

"Grieve not, O king. Raise another army."

"I lost my fortune when I lost my army."

"King," said Anathapindika, "I shall give you the gold you need, and you will be victorious."

Prasenajit sprang to his feet.

"You have saved me, Anathapindika!" he exclaimed. "I am grateful."

With Anathapindika's gold, Prasenajit raised a formidable host. He marched against Ajatasatru.

When the two armies met, the din terrified the Gods themselves. Prasenajit used a battle array he had been taught by men from a distant land. He attacked swiftly; Ajatasatru had no defense. He, in turn, was defeated, and he was captured.

"Kill me," he cried to Prasenajit.

"I shall spare your life," said Prasenajit. "I shall take you to the Blessed Master, and he will decide your fate."

The Master had recently arrived at Jeta's park. Prasenajit said to him:

"Behold, O Blessed One! King Ajatasatru is my prisoner. He hates me, though I bear him no ill will. He attacked me, for some trivial reason, and defeated me at first, but now he is at my mercy. I do not wish to kill him, O Blessed One. For the sake of his father, Vimbasara, who was my friend, I would like to set him free."

"Then set him free," said the Master. "Victory begets hatred; defeat begets suffering. They that are wise will forgo both victory and defeat. Insult is born of insult, anger of anger. They that are wise will forgo both victory and defeat. Every murderer is struck down by a murderer; every conqueror is struck down by a conqueror. They that are wise will forgo both victory and defeat."

In the presence of the Master, Ajatasatru promised to be a faithful friend to Prasenajit.

"And," he added, "let us be more than friends. I have a son, as you know, and you have a daughter, Kshema, who is still unmarried. Will you give your daughter to my son?"

"So be it," said Prasenajit. "And may this

happy marriage be the earnest of our happy friendship."

The Master approved. The two kings ever after lived at peace with each other, and Ajatasatru became known for his gentleness.

14

THE Master was growing old. When he was in Rajagriha, he called the monks together, and he spoke to them at great length:

"Monks, do not forget the precepts I have given you. Observe them carefully. You will assemble twice a month, and you will confess your transgressions to one another. If you feel that you have done evil, and you keep it to yourself, you will be guilty of a lie. Admit your transgressions: the confession will bring you rest and peace. The four gravest sins a monk can commit are, as you know: to have intercourse with a woman; to steal anything whatsoever; to kill a human being or instigate a murder; and to pretend to possess a superhuman power that he knows he does not possess. A monk who has committed one of these four sins must be expelled from the community. Monks, do not bandy words with women, and do not corrupt them. Do not bear false witness against your brothers. Do not try to sow discord in the community. Do not strive to evade a reprimand. Never lie, and insult no one. Observe carefully, O monks, all the precepts I have given you."

He said further:

"Seriousness is the province of immortality; frivolity, the province of death. They that are serious do not die; they that are frivolous are always dead. Therefore would the wise be serious. The wise attain the supreme blessing, nirvana. He sees his glory increase who is energetic and can remember, who thinks honestly and acts deliberately, who is continent, who lives within the law, and who is serious. It is frivolity the fools and the weakminded pursue; the wise treasure seriousness as a miser his gold. The monk who would be serious, who sees the danger of frivolity, shakes the evil law like the wind does the leaves; he tears asunder the bonds that bind him to the world; he is close to nirvana. Standing on the terrace of wisdom, released from all suffering, the serious man who has conquered frivolity looks out over the unhappy multitude, as, from the summit of a mountain, one might gaze upon the crowd in the plains below."

15

BEFORE he died, the Blessed One decided to go on a long journey. He wanted to visit certain of his disciples and exhort them to observe his teachings with scrupulous care. With only Ananda for a companion, he left the city óf Rajagriha.

One day, while he was resting in the corner of a field, he said to Ananda:

"There will come a time when men will wonder why I once entered a woman's womb. They will question the perfect purity of my birth, and they will doubt whether I ever had supreme power. These benighted men will never understand that, for him who devotes his life to works of holiness, the body is free from the impurity of birth. He who would seek supreme knowledge must enter a woman's womb; he must, out of pity for mankind, be born into the world of men. For if he were a God, how could he set in motion the wheel of the law? Imagine the Buddha as a God, Ananda; men would soon lose heart. They would say, 'The Buddha, who is a God, has happiness, holiness, perfection; but we, how can we hope to attain them?'

And they would be in deep despair. Oh, let them keep still, these benighted creatures! Let them not try to steal the law, for they would use it ill. Rather, let them consider the Buddha's nature incomprehensible, these men who will never be able to gauge my eminence!"

A shepherd was crossing the field. He had the serenity of a man who is quietly performing a labor of joy.

"Who are you, shepherd?" the Master asked him.

"My name is Dhaniya," replied the shepherd.

"Where are you going?" asked the Master.

"I am going home to my wife and childreh."

"You seem to know pure happiness, shepherd?"

"I have boiled my rice, I have milked my cows," said the shepherd Dhaniya; "I live with my family on the banks of the river; my house is well roofed, my fire is lighted; so fall if you will, O rain of the sky."

"I am rid of anger, I am rid of stubbornness," said the Master; "I bide for a night on the banks of the river; my house has no roof, the fire of passions is quenched in my being; so fall if you will, O rain of the sky."

"The gadflies never torment my herd," said the shepherd Dhaniya; "my cows roam in the grassy meadows; they can abide the coming rain; so fall if you will, O rain of the sky."

"I built a sturdy raft, I set sail for nirvana," said the Master; "I crossed the torrent of passions and I reached the saintly shores; I need the raft no longer; so fall if you will, O rain of the sky."

"My wife is obedient, she is chaste and good," said the shepherd Dhaniya; "she has lived with me these many years; she is pleasant and kindly, no one speaks ill of her; so fall if you will, O rain of the sky."

"My mind is obedient, it is loosed from all bonds," said the Master; "I have trained it these many years; it is quite docile, no evil is left in me; so fall if you will, O rain of the sky."

"I myself pay my servants their wages," said the shepherd Dhaniya; "my children receive wholesome food at my board; no one has ever tried to speak ill of them; so fall if you will, O rain of the sky."

"I am the servant of no one," said the Master; "with what I earn I travel the whole world; there is for me no need of a servant; so fall if you will, O rain of the sky."

"I have cows, I have calves, I have heifers," said the shepherd Dhaniya, "and I have a dog that is lord of my herd; so fall if you will, O rain of the sky."

"I have neither cows nor calves nor heifers,"

said the Master, "and I have no dog to be on guard; so fall if you will, O rain of the sky."

"The stakes are driven deep in the ground, nothing can move them," said the shepherd Dhaniya; "the ropes are new and made of strong grasses; the cows will never break them now; so fall if you will, O rain of the sky."

"Like the dog that has broken his chain," said the Master, "like the elephant that has broken his shackles, never again will I enter a womb; so fall if you will, O rain of the sky."

The shepherd Dhaniya bowed before the Master and said:

"I know now who you are, O Blessed One; come with me to my home."

As they were about to enter the house, the rain fell in torrents and formed little streams that trickled over the ground. When Dhaniya heard the rain, he spoke these words:

"Verily, we have acquired great riches since we have seen the Buddha. O Master, you are our refuge, you who have looked at us with the eyes of wisdom. Be our protector, O Saint! We are obedient, my wife and I; if we lead a life of holiness, we shall conquer birth and death, and we shall have done with suffering."

Then a voice was heard, and Mara, the Evil One,

stood before them. No one had seen him come.

"He who has sons is happy to see his sons," said Mara, the Evil One; "he who has cows is happy to see his cows; happy is the man of substance, and he who has no substance has no happiness."

"He who has sons is worried to see his sons," said the Master; "he who has cows is worried to see his cows; worried is the man of substance, and he who has no substance has no worries."

But Mara had fled. Dhaniya and his wife were listening to the Master speak.

16

THE Master came to the banks of the Ganges, to the place where the city of Pataliputra was being built. He bowed before the walls that were beginning to rise out of the ground, and he exclaimed:

"This city will one day have greatness and renown; many heroes will be born here, here will reign a famous king. A thriving city you will be, O Pataliputra, and down through the ages men will praise your name."

He crossed the river. He set out for Vaisali, but in the village of Bailva he became gravely ill. He suffered intense pain. Ananda wept, for he thought he was dying. But the Master remembered the many disciples he had still to visit; he did not wish to enter nirvana until he had given them final instructions. By the strength of his will, he overcame the sickness, and life did not leave him. He recovered.

When he was well again, he went outside the house that had given him shelter, and he took a seat that had been prepared for him near the door. Ananda came and sat down beside him.

"My Lord," said he, "I see that you have recovered your health. When I found you so ill, my strength failed me; I was faint. There were times I could not realize that the Master was sick. And yet I was reassured, for I remembered that you had not disclosed your intentions regarding the community, and I knew you would not enter nirvana without first revealing them."

The Blessed One spoke these words:

"What more does the community want of me, Ananda? I have stated the doctrine, and I have taught it; there is not a single point I have not expounded! Let him who thinks, 'I want to rule over the community,' disclose his intentions regarding the community. The Blessed One, Ananda, never thought, 'I want to rule over the community.' Why then should he disclose his intentions? I am an old man, Ananda; my hair is white, and I have grown feeble. I am eighty years old; I have come to the end of the road. Be, now, each one of you, your own torch; look to no one to bring you light. He who is his own torch, after I have left the world, will show that he has understood the meaning of my words; he will be my true disciple, Ananda; he will know the right way to live."

He set out again, and presently he arrived at Vaisali. He went through the city, begging his food from door to door. Suddenly, he saw Mara standing before him.

"The hour has come," said the Evil One; "enter nirvana, O Blessed One."

"No," replied the Buddha. "I know when I must enter nirvana; I know better than you, Evil One. A few months more, and it will be time. Three months more, and the Blessed One will enter nirvana."

At these words the earth shook, and thunder rolled across the sky: the Blessed One had destroyed the will by which he still held to life; he had set the time for his entry into nirvana. The earth shook, and thunder rolled across the sky.

In the evening he assembled the monks of Vaisali, and he addressed them.

"O monks, preserve carefully, the knowledge I have acquired and that I have taught you, and walk in the right path, in order that the life of holiness may long endure, for the joy and salvation of the world, for the joy and salvation of the Gods, for the joy and salvation of mankind. A few months more, and my time will have come; three months more, and I shall enter nirvana. I go and you remain. But never cease to struggle, O monks. He who falters not in the path of truth avoids birth, avoids death, for ever and ever avoids suffering."

THE LIFE OF BUDDHA

The following day, he again wandered through the city, in quest of alms; then, with a few disciples, he set out on the road to Kusinagara, where he had decided to enter nirvana.

П

THE Master and his disciples stopped at Pava, in the garden of Cunda, the blacksmith. Cunda came and paid homage to the Master, and said to him:

"My Lord, do me the honor of taking your meal at my home, to-morrow."

The Master accepted. The next day, Cunda had pork and other delicacies prepared for his guests. They arrived and took their seats. When the Master saw the pork, he pointed to it and said:

"No one but me could eat that, Cunda; you must keep it for me. My disciples will partake of the other delicacies."

When he had eaten, he said:

"Bury deep in the ground what I have left untouched; the Buddha alone can eat of such meat."

Then he left. The disciples followed.

They had gone only a short distance from Pava when the Master began to feel weary and sick. Ananda grieved, and he cursed Cunda, the blacksmith, for having offered the Master this fatal meal.

"Ananda," said the Master, "do not be angry

with Cunda, the blacksmith. Great rewards are re-
served to him for the food he gave me. Of all the
meals I have ever had, two are most deserving of
praise: the one that Sujata, and the other that
Cunda, the blacksmith, served to me."

He overcame his weariness and presently he
reached the banks of the Kakutstha. The river was
peaceful and pure. The Master bathed in the limpid waters. After the bath, he drank, then went
to a mango grove. There, he said to the monk
Cundaka:

"Fold my cloak in four, that I may lie down and
rest."

Cundaka cheerfully obeyed. He quickly folded
the cloak in four and spread it on the ground. The
Master lay down, and Cundaka sat beside him.

The Master rested a few hours. Then he set out
again, and he finally arrived at Kusinagara. There,
on the banks of the Hiranyavati, stood a pleasant,
peaceful little wood.

The Master said:

"Go, Ananda, and prepare a couch for me between two twin trees. Have the head to the north.
I am ill, Ananda."

Ananda prepared the couch, and the Master
went and reclined on it.

18

IT was not the season for trees to bloom, yet the two trees that sheltered the Master were covered with blossoms. The flowers fell gently upon his couch, and from the sky, sweet melodies slowly drifted down.

The Master said to pious Ananda:

"See: it is not the season for flowers, yet these trees have bloomed, and the blossoms are raining down upon me. Listen: the air is joyous with the songs that the happy Gods are singing in the sky in honor of the Buddha. But the Buddha is paid a more enduring honor than this. Monks, nuns, believers, all those who see the truth, all those who live within the law, they are the ones that do the Buddha supreme honor. Therefore you must live according to the law, Ananda, and, even in the most trivial matters, you must follow the sacred path of truth."

Ananda was weeping. He walked away, to hide his tears.

He thought, "For many misdeeds I have not yet been forgiven, and I shall be guilty of many more